THE
BIRTH OF
A CHRISTIAN

MARGARET L. BlANChARd

To Evelyn L. Morris Thanks for your support and for your "home". We hope you enjoy the book half as Much as we enjoy the house Margaret Blanchard '98

Published by
Milligan Books

Book Formatting
By Chris Ebuehi - Graphic Options

Published and Distributed by:
Milligan Books
an imprint of
Professional Business Consultants
2108 W. Manchester, Suite C,
Los Angeles, California 90047
(213) 750-3592

First Printing, January, 1998
10 9 8 7 6 5 4 3 2 1

ISBN 1 881524-15-9

My friend, I stand in the judgment and feel that you are to blame somehow.

On earth I walked with you day by day and never did you point the way.

You knew the Lord in truth and glory, but never did you tell the story.

My knowledge of him was very dim, you could have led me safely to Him.

We walked day by day and talked by night and yet you showed me not the light.

You let me live, and love, and die. You knew I'd never live on high.

Yes, I called you friend in life and trusted you through joy and strife. And yet on

coming to the end I cannot now call you "my friend."

Author unknown

Dedication

To my divinely chosen partner for life, Lt. Col. Larry Donell Blanchard, Esq. : There are not enough adjectives to give my husband the adulation he deserves for all the contributions he made to this book. However, his loving support, quiet tolerance of the things that went undone and steadfast faith in my ability to create were all given freely as I worked on the drafting and research for this book. He never complained when the space beside him in bed was empty as I slipped out of bed in the middle of many nights and went downstairs to work. He tiptoed around letting me sleep late the next morning while he prepared to go to work. Without his patience and understanding, I am sure I would not have been as tuned in to the Spirit as I was while I worked. *The Birth of a Christian* as a completed work owes much of its life to Larry. After affording me the privilege to explore my creative abilities, he unselfishly took care of the little things that I did not always have time to do within the house. He always worked with me and assisted me whenever I needed him. Sometimes he solicited the help of others when there were problems we could not solve concerning the input of data for the manuscript.

When the pressure to finish became almost overwhelming, he stepped in and began to edit my work as he edits legal documents, with a fine toothed comb. When I needed to change from Word Perfect to Microsoft Word, (I was not at all familiar with the latter) he agreed to make the transition for me. He even taught me how to work in the new program along with him. While we worked side by side, he provided a spiritual atmosphere for us to work. Larry had secured a tape with good spiritual instrumentals like, Amazing Grace, Sweet Hour of Prayer, Rock of Ages, Just as I Am and many other inspirational songs. A female vocalist narrated the spiritual meaning of life with God on the tape while this wonderful music played in the background. We felt the anointing that was upon her as she spoke. Night after night, he came home from work and began to work with me immediately after dinner. Each night we listened to praise songs from that tape as we worked. The Spirit filled the room and thus filled us.

I humbly dedicate this book to my husband with much love, respect, sincerity and the blessings that I am sure God has in store for him for his kindness and sensitivity.

Acknowledgments

I acknowledge the guidance and the love of the Spirit of God for enabling me to write as he directed me. To the Lord God Almighty for keeping me through all the changes I underwent while writing *The Birth of A Christian*, I give praise and glory forever.

A very special thanks to my family for their love and support, especially my sisters, Mary Crump and Sadie Burrell. Mary prayed with and for me from the moment I told her I was commissioned to write a book. Later she pushed, pulled and prodded me to finish. Finally she gave me a deadline that motivated me to work hard to try to meet. Perhaps without her deadline, the book would not have been completed in a timely manner. Her encouragement played an intricate part in the finished product.

Sadie listened to the beginnings of chapter after chapter as we talked between Georgia and Nevada. As an avid reader, she gave me some valuable advice from a reader's perspective that kept me on the right path as a reader, when I began to write in a way that pleased me. Her prayers were endless.

My prayer partner, my friend, my sister in the Lord, Lisa Artis who was always there, hands on. As new ideas unfolded, I tested them on Lisa before I incorporated them in the book. She always took time to listen and give unbiased input. She prayed for me constantly and with me weekly.

Rosie Milligan Ph.D., long time friend (and new publisher for me), agreed to publish the book sight unseen. As

Mary's deadline approached, Rosie became like a pinch hitter in a baseball game. She stepped up to the plate and said; "Send me the manuscript and I will do my best." The most wonderful man I know, my husband, Larry Blanchard who did everything except co-author the book. I must admit, he did add his *signature* to a few phrases. His support, which was crucial to my ability to work in a pleasant, peaceful environment, was never missing.

Author's Preface

The *Birth of a Christian* is an introductory journey through life. It will take readers from life as a sinner to the new birth and through some of the major steps necessary for the birth of a Christian to take place within the heart of believers. It will take readers up memory lane with Jesus as he traveled from heaven to earth, to the cross and back to heaven again. What he gave up, what he endured and why he did all of this will be visited briefly.

This book was designed to give readers an idea of some of the didactics of being born anew into Christ and what it takes to become a Christian. It parallels the birth, the growth and life sustaining processes of new born infants and children in the natural to new born infants and children of the Spirit. It was written to give young believers an inspired view of some of the things they can expect to encounter as they *begin to grow-up* in the Lord. *The Birth of a Christian* was written to inform infant and beginning believers that the change from one lifestyle to another is progressive. Although the lives of infants in the natural and the lives of spiritual infants are similar in many ways, they are very different in other important ways.

I wanted to simplify the birth, growth and developmental process for new believers and point out the unequivocal importance of going through the stages of development in a manner that has been divinely pre-organized. This book is not meant to preach to or at sinners or new believers but to give a fresh, simple approach to the Christian experience. Hopefully someone will be motivated to make a life changing transition after reading this book. There are probably many unanswered *"how to"* questions in the minds of many infant believers and more *"Christians ought to do"* commands than they are capable of handling. In this book some of those questions may be answered. I know that not knowing where to begin kept me in infancy for a longer time than necessary. I believe many young believers are still wandering in the wilderness of spiritual ignorance. They do not know what to do, where to go nor how to get where they need to be in order to live the life of a Christian. This book will, by no means, answer all those questions. However, it is my desire to point readers to a place where the answers may be found.

When I began to write this book, I had some ideas of what I wanted to put in it and they were not all God ordained. I wrote draft after draft but nothing seemed to fit right. I put the entire manuscript aside for a while and then picked it up again when I was ready to listen to the Spirit. I was challenged by the adversary in numerous ways as he unsuccessfully attempted to prevent me from writing this book. I developed strange pains in strange places like my fingers when I tried to type and my legs when I tried to sit. Finally I asked the Lord if he wanted me to write a book. His Answer was; "No, I want to use you to write a book for me." While I was writing the many drafts it took before this book was formed, I learned many life changing lessons as I searched the Scriptures, prayed and did other research. I learned to submit to the Lord and permit him to do his work through me. I am excited as I endeavor to share some of my experiences with you. This book is what I believe God wanted me to write. I hope you will find something that will change your life and motivate you to continue to grow in the Lord as you read *The Birth of a Christian* with an open mind. I know that the Lord wanted to create a newness within me before he permitted me to present anything to my readers. If he did this within me, I am certain he can do it within you. I now know that many of the principles work because I have tried some of them for myself. Now I challenge you to put some of them to the test. I took the liberty to paraphrase some of the Scriptures upon the urging of the Holy Spirit. I suggest readers verify the Scriptures for themselves. Each time I read the same passage of Scripture, I gain more wisdom from it than I did upon reading it before. God speaks to the hearts of individuals but he and his word never changes.

The purpose of this book is to act in obedience to the Lord and to share with others who may be struggling with no definite plan of action. I hope some of your needs will be met as you read it.

THE BIRTH OF A CHRISTIAN

Contents

THE BIRTH OF A CHRISTIAN

Chapter One

THE PROCESS AND THE PLAN

We have all, at some point and time, wondered why we were born, what purpose we are to fulfill and when we will learn what we are supposed to do with our lives. We were created for the purpose of loving God, communicating with him and serving him. All these things he has already done for us. However, we were all born with sinful hearts, causing us to be dead in sins and trespasses. Before we can begin to experience God's love, we must be born again and given new hearts and a new nature. This new birth, which is totally different from the natural birth, is perfect, without any defects because the one who made it possible was perfect. It took an emotional, extremely painful, humiliating experience for the new birth of just one sinner to take place. A love sacrifice by someone without sin was the requirement. There was no such person on the face of the earth. God, in his mercy, gave us his only begotten Son as the ultimate sacrifice to pay for the sins of the world. Jesus willingly became that sacrifice because of his great love for the Father.

Jesus was on his mighty throne in glory with the Father. He left the majesty of royalty in the highest form and went through the same natural birth process everyone else experiences. This great king was born in a barn with farm animals in attendance. He donned flesh and grew up as a human boy and was subjected to the training of his earthly parents. He shared in our human pains and our human emotions. As he grew up and began the work he came here to do, he was tempted by Satan, ridiculed and persecuted by his own people, the ones he came here to save from the consequences and the curse of sin. He did not let them get under his skin. He called some disciples, taught them by precept and example, so that his works would continue through mankind. He submitted himself to death on the cross. That was the most humiliating way for a criminal to die but Jesus, who committed no crime, submitted to such a death. Why? Jesus submitted to such a death in order for the birth of a Christian to become a reality for everyone on earth. All this so that you and I could have the opportunity to fulfill God's purpose for creating us.

Roman soldiers treated him terribly. They embedded thorns deep into his forehead and all around his head. As they forced the thorns to adhere to his skull, his skin was torn in several places, causing rivets of blood to stream down his face. They made a cross of green four by fours and put it on Jesus' back and made him carry it up a hill in the heat of the day. As he walked up that hill with that heavy cross, they whipped him across his back with leather straps that broke the skin on his back causing more bloodshed. None of us can imagine the agony of such dreadful pain. When Jesus finally reached the top of the hill, after falling down under the weight of the cross several times, they took the cross and laid it down on the ground. They stretched Jesus out on it like a lamb being prepared for a sacrifice, and nailed blunt edged nails into the palms of his hands and his feet to secure him to the cross. Then they lifted the cross up, with the body of Jesus attached. Only those familiar with his teachings knew that he had said; "But I, when I am lifted up from the earth, will draw all men to myself" (according to John 12:32).

Jesus did not have to endure any of that wretchedness. At any time during the course of his agony, he could have commanded legions of angels to come to his rescue. But he was faithful and obedient. He went all the way, knowing he had to complete the job he came here to do. He refused to leave us at the mercy of Satan. The Roman soldiers and many of the Israelites did not believe he was the Christ. Many people today, still do not believe he is the Christ, to their disadvantage. While he was going through the worst time of his life, the Father turned his face away from him because his eyes are too pure to look on sin. Jesus was bearing all the sins of the world; past, present and future. He had only said the things that were necessary to fulfill the Scriptures so far. However, the separation from his Father, from whom he had never been separated, caused pain within his inner being. He cried out in a loud voice; "Father, Father, why have you forsaken me?" Then he hung his head and died in the flesh. After his death, the Roman soldiers still tried to torture him. They pierced him in his side with a sword and that precious, life-giving, purified blood came streaming down. No one had ever been born again at that time. We were all still dead in trespasses and sin and still without a covenant relationship with God, but Jesus made it possible for us to be made alive through sacrificial love. His death made it possible for our sins to be forgiven. Now we can be set free from the curse that sin had imposed upon us. The sins, the condemnation and the curse were all nailed to the cross with Jesus. Jesus did not stop acting on our behalf on the cross. He descended to hell and took the keys of death and the grave from Satan and disarmed him and his demons, who entice people to follow false teachings about Christ (according to Colossians 2: 13-15).

Now the new birth can take place within anyone because of what Jesus did for us. Many processes and procedures go on behind the scenes when the nature of a sinner is changed. He is *regenerated,* which is the actual act of being born again. No one can enter the kingdom of God unless he is purified or born of the water (the living water which is Jesus) and equipped for holiness by being born of the Spirit (according to John 3:16). When the process of *reconciliation* takes place it establishes peace between God and man and man and God. This was made possible by the atoning work of Jesus on the cross. We were still his enemies yet he reconciled us to God by not counting our sins against us (according to 2 Corinthians 5:19). It was an *at-one-ness process* making it possible for us to be one with him and the Father. We are not reconciled to God until we accept the provisions he made for our salvation. We are *redeemed* at this time because Jesus paid the full price to set us free from the bondage and the curse of sin. We were prisoners to sin, sitting on death row, having been condemned to die and suffer the consequences that follow sin. Jesus shed his blood and sacrificed his life in the flesh for our freedom. Those who were sitting in the darkness of those jail cells of life, controlled by sin, were given the message of redemption (according to Acts 26:18). This message could rescue them from the power of Satan and motivate them to turn to God and be brought into the light. The judicial or legal act of releasing sinners from condemnation and restoring them to the place of divine favor man had with God before the fall, called *Justification,* occurs during the new birth. Justification differs from regeneration in that it changes our *relationship* to God. Regeneration changes our *nature* by the power of the Holy Spirit. The *adoption* is an act of unmerited love by a loving Father, it takes place when we put on his Son Jesus Christ, and become his again.

    Sanctification and *conversion* are intricate components of the new birth, however, they do not usually occur at the time of the new birth. Sanctification is the setting apart from sin and profanity for sacred purpose. It is the carrying forward of the work of grace in the soul to its completion. Sanctification involves the will of God working in the life of believers. For God's perfect will to prevail, man has to surrender his own will. *Conversion* is the change that takes place when believers no longer permit the natural nature to control the spiritual nature at any time in any form. They turn away from sin completely and turn towards God completely and actually hate every wrong thought, deed or path taken. The Psalmist had the conversion idea when he said; One thing I ask of the Lord, this is what I will seek; That I may dwell in the house of the Lord all the days of my life, to gaze upon the beauty of the Lord and seek him in his temple (27:4). New born believers are not usually equipped with enough divine knowledge, wisdom and understanding to turn away from their former lifestyles and live the life necessary for sanctification and conversion to come to pass. Of course it is not impossible because nothing is impossible with the Lord. How ready were you to make the complete change and be totally separated from the world and its practices when you were first born anew? How ready do you think you are you right now?

The new birth is a spiritual process, unlike the birth of a natural infant. The lives of the two have many similarities though. Both are innocent of all the dangers that await them in the world. They are dependent creatures, needing someone to feed them and care for them so that they may grow. Both can only digest small feedings of food consistent with their delicate digestive systems. Without a caretaker, they can do anything to enhance their growth and development. If they are not properly fed and nurtured, both will develop Failure to Thrive Syndrome. Natural born infants usually require medical intervention, if they are to thrive when they are cursed with this syndrome. Natural born infants see their parents or caretaker as gods. They believe whatever they say without doubting their ability to carry out their proposed plans. They feel safe and comfortable when they are in the presence of loving caretakers. They watch them closely and attempt to mimic whatever they see and hear them do.

Spiritual believers all begin their lives as infants no mat-

5

ter what chronological age they were when they received their new nature. Our Father and our caretaker are both divine. Our Father left us in the capable hands of the Holy Spirit to care for us from birth throughout eternity. He is always available to guide us in the right direction, to teach us whatever we need to know about our new lives and to mold us in accordance with the will of our Father. We are to watch the life of our Savior carefully, and like spiritually new born infants, take on the traits he characterized throughout his life. We cannot become functional believers without the Father, the Son and the Holy Spirit. While we are permitted to keep our family members we were born with in the natural, we gain access into the new, royal family of God. Now we are to act like royalty.

God is so gracious and merciful, until he permits everyone, everywhere to be born again. He does not care how filthy you are or how deeply embedded in sin you have fallen, he assures you that the blood of Jesus is still powerful enough to make you pure. The adversary does not want to lose your devotion so he will either attempt to prevent you from coming to Jesus or destroy your hope of ever being made pure. He may try both because that's what he does best, prevent and destroy. Jesus tells us he came so *you* could have life more abundantly than you ever knew was possible. *Everyone* has sinned and failed to bring glory to God with their lives. That is the very reason Jesus went to Calvary with that heavy cross. God still loves you and he wants you to come to him and reason with him about your sins (according to Isiah 1: 18). They may be red like crimson because of the blood on your hands. The blood of Jesus can wash every one of your sins and they will come out as white as new snow. When the Lord set us free from sin along with its curse, there will be no stains of our former sins left. Sinners are not only welcome to come to Jesus, they are invited by the Father. You can be born again of the Spirit of the living God no matter what state you are in. One thing he requires of sinners and that is repentance.

Among the first sermons Jesus preached after he began his ministry was; "Repent or perish." He wants us to change the course of our present lives so that we can take the course plotted out for all believers by the Father. Conception of the new life begins with repentance. No one *can* change the course of his life without divine intervention but we must not resist the idea and reject the message. Jesus, who embodies the kingdom of God, is near when the sermon of repentance is being preached. The Holy Spirit is ready to enable anyone who is willing to have the course of his life changed. As we know, many things take place when a sinner is made new. The spiritual *operating room* is always ready to deliver a sinner from his ways. Natural mothers-to-be take an active part in the delivery of their new born infants. The Father, the Son and the Holy Spirit all take an active part in the delivery of each believer. If sinners know just who the Father is and believe he is who he says he is, deliverance can become imminent. *How will* sinners know God and where will they get enough faith to believe he is who he says he is? All this has been pre-planned.

Jesus tells his hearers that no one *can* come to him unless the Father draws them and he will raise them up on the last day (according to John 6: 44-45). He tells us; "They will *all be* taught by God." Everyone who listens to the Father learns from him to come to Jesus. God has made it possible for everyone whom he draws to believe and know how to come to Jesus. Consequently, faith comes by hearing the message, and the message is heard through the word of Christ (according to Romans 10: 16). What is the message? It is the gospel of Jesus Christ. He came in the flesh. He walked among men, teaching them by precept and example. He underwent the horrors of Calvary before he died for our sins. He was buried in a borrowed tomb. On the third day he rose just as he promised his disciples he would. He ascended into heaven where he now abides with all power over heaven and earth in his hands. This message is not limited to preachers and evangelists. God knows everyone will not go anywhere to hear the message. That's why he sends his messengers to the people. He uses ordinary people like you and me.

A few months ago I went on a business trip with my husband. I really did not want to go but he was persistent and I gave in. We had reservations at an *inn* as opposed to the four star hotels we usually stayed in during his business trips. There were no shops, no gym and nothing of interest within walking distance. My husband needed the car for business so I was stuck in the room with nothing to do but write. An extremely young looking female came to clean our room. I was extremely concerned for her in the line of work she was doing. When she finished her task I was prompted to tip her. As I searched for money, we began to talk. I expressed my concerns to her. She assured me she was twenty-one years old and a junior in college but was forced to drop out because she could no longer afford to attend. I asked her if she knew how to pray. She gave me a bored, questioning look and shook her head in the negative. I asked her if she had been born again. The look she gave me was more quizzical than the previous one. Finally she responded; "I go to church with my mother and my aunt sometimes and read the Bible a little." I was inspired to tell her about the gospel and the plan the Lord had for her life. I told her about the prayers of those who belong to him and how he cared for his own. I gave her the plan of salvation and wrote down specific Scripture for her to read, underlining Romans 10: 9-10. Her face lit up and she hugged me as she left the room smiling. She told me; "You made my day." As soon as I closed the door the Spirit whispered; "This is how the Father draws sinners to him." He will provide a means for sinners to hear the message and respond to the message. Believers are used as his messengers when we avail ourselves to him.

His messengers never know how he is going to work in the

hearts of those whom he draws. We are to be obedient and do *exactly* as the Spirit leads us to do, no more and no less. Sometimes we want to see the fruit of our labors. I wanted to lead that young lady into the prayer of repentance and salvation but the Spirit was explicit in what he wanted me to do. Knowing and respecting God's sovereignty in that he does what he wants just as he has planned it, I was obedient. Recognizing and respecting his sovereignty is counted as obedience.

The new birth is a free gift of love, offered to everyone at some point and time in the span of a lifetime. Jesus is the *only* way sinners can be redeemed and set free from the prison of sin. The new birth is divinely administered by the Godhead who are all divine. That love gift is the Son of God, Jesus Christ, an eternal gift of mercy and grace. Refusal to accept salvation is seen as rejecting God's Son and counting his Calvary experience as dung. Those who reject Jesus Christ cannot escape the just and righteous judgment of God. They will not know God and cannot respond to him in obedience. Their understanding will be darkened and they will be punished with everlasting destruction. They will be shut out from the presence of the Lord and the majesty of his power forever (according to 2 Thessalonians 1: 8, 9). Jesus is the one and only way to salvation or the new birth and salvation is the *only* way sinners can be delivered from the bondage of Satan.

Jesus said; "I am the way the truth and the life, no one comes to the Father except through me" (according to John 14: 6). The pathway that leads to the completed process of salvation is small and narrow and unfortunately, not many people will find it. The masses will enter life though the broad and wide gate leading to destruction (according to Matthew 7: 13). Jesus' willingness to leave his throne in glory to come to a world controlled by wickedness and deceitfulness was not without a purpose. Now all power in heaven and earth has been handed over to him. He is the gate through which everyone who inherits eternal life must pass. God is not trying to make deliverance hard. On the contrary, he has made all the provisions for it to come to pass. All sinners have to do is receive the gift he is offering and have a *desire* to let him change them. It is not God's will that anyone should perish, he is patient, wanting everyone to come to repentance (according to 2 Peter 3: 9).

Because God created us as free moral agents, with the ability to make our own decisions independent of him, anyone can choose to accept or reject the gift. What we are accepting is a package deal filled with wonderful, life changing benefits. We get the Father, the Son and the Holy Spirit, new hearts, the promises in the word of God and so much more than our minds have room to imagine. By rejecting Jesus Christ, sinners will get a free ticket to spend eternity in hell and be tormented forever and ever.

Have you reached out to receive the gift and become partakers of all the benefits that comes with the gift? Salvation is a voluntary, conscious, confession of one's belief in the gospel. Dedication as a child is an involuntary act and cannot be accepted in lieu of salvation. Water baptism cannot deliver sinners from the curse of sin. Church membership and church works are in vain unless there has been a personal confession of faith. All of these things are equivalent to making an attempt to enter the kingdom of God another way except through Jesus Christ. That is impossible. Failure to enter by the door of Jesus Christ will lead to hell and destruction. Are you sure of where you will spend eternity? Maybe the Father is drawing you to his Son now. Do not harden your heart as some did and paid for their decision with their lives.

Many church members, working in high places within the organized church, have not received Jesus in their lives yet. Some still believe they will be saved because of their good works. I organized a New Membership Orientation class a few years ago. The class I taught was for members joining church with a letter from their previous church outlining their good works and those who claimed to have *Christian experience.* I opened each new class by asking everyone who knew where they were spending eternity to raise their hands. At first, I was surprised to find that almost all of the joining members were unaware of the plan of salvation. Many either did not know or did not believe Jesus when he said he would raise up those whom the Father drew to him on the last day. There were deacons, a few preachers, choir members, trustees and workers from every organization within the church in my class. The first order of business was to give the plan of salvation and lend assistance to those who wanted to make a personal commitment. Many received Jesus as Lord in my class. Others were too ashamed but later told me they made the commitment at home.

I tell you, now is the time of God's favor, now is the time of salvation. I urge you not to receive God's grace in vain. In the time of his favor he heard us and in the day of salvation he helped us (according to 2 Corinthians 6: 1, 2). The chance to accept Jesus as your Savior may not come again. Remember, salvation is not for this life only, it's eternal (according to Hebrews 5: 9). On the basis of the perfection of Jesus through temptations, sufferings and humiliation, he became the source of eternal salvation for all who obey him. Obey his voice and come today. The word is already near you, which is the word of faith. If you confess with your mouth, "Jesus is Lord," and believe in your heart that God raised him from the dead, you will be saved. It is with your heart that you believe and are justified and it is with your mouth that you confess and are saved (according to Romans 10: 8-10). No one can say "Jesus is Lord," except by the Holy Spirit (according to I Corinthians 12: 3). It is the Holy Spirit that enables sinners to make the confession as the Father directs him.

Everyone who becomes children of God through the new birth will be known of the Savior. Those who go through the motions upon the advice of someone else, or pretend to be believers when they are not, will be punished. The Lord knows who belongs to him and who does not, even if mankind is fooled by the acts of pretending. When the Son of man comes for his own he will separate true believers from deceivers. He will say to the deceivers; "Depart from me, you who are cursed, into the eternal fire prepared for the devil and his angels (according to Matthew 25: 41)." Once we come to the Son, we can never be snatched out of his hand. He is able to keep us throughout eternity because the Father who gave us to him is greater than all. He has already given eternal life to his children (according to John 10: 28, 29).

If you have not made the commitment, now may be your time to accept the gift of salvation. If you don't know how to do it, here is an example: Pray; "Lord, I am sorry for my sins. I want to turn around and go in a different direction. I confess," "Jesus is Lord," and I believe God raised him from the dead. I accept your invitation and believe that upon my confession you came into my life to live forever. I thank you Jesus, Amen.

You may not feel differently after your confession. Salvation is not based on feelings but on the word of God. It is by God's kindness and forgiving love that you were saved, through faith. This was not of you, but it was a gift from God (according to Ephesians 2: 8). There was nothing any of us could have done to merit such love. Some people have remarkable experiences during the transition phase. How we respond does not effect the work the Holy Spirit does within us. I had an indelible experience that made an eternal impression on my mind at the time of my new birth.

I was ten years old and wanted to be saved. We lived in Memphis, Tennessee at the time. My parents were very firm in their refusal to permit us to go before the church and shake the preacher's hand saying we wanted to be baptized. They insisted we go to the rural area of Tennessee, called the country. My older sister, Mary and I were sent to spend time with our aunt and uncle during the revival. We were told to cease all playing and joking and seriously pray; "Lord, forgive me of my sins and save my soul," continuously until our prayers were answered. At church we were placed on the Mourners Bench (a row of seats in the front part of the church) along with other children. The saints sang and prayed for our salvation during revival. On the very first night a few children began to jump up from the bench and shout. The saints surrounded them shouting out, "Confess him, confess him!" I looked up and saw that my sister, Mary had jumped up and was shouting! I thought: "This is the last straw, she should be ashamed of herself." I had no intentions of carrying out in such uncivilized manner. That Monday during noon revival as the saints sang and prayed, I began to feel an involuntary stirring deep within my inner being. I did not know what it was but I folded my arms as tight as I could across my chest so this movement would not take control of me. I must have lost control because all of a sudden, I felt as if I were timeless and weightless as I began to travel. Seemingly, I entered into another dimension in time and space. At first it was very dark, but I was not afraid. I felt rather peaceful. I seem to have been traveling through a tunnel like maze. Before I reached the opening, I saw a bright, white light. Gentle hands seemed to have deposited me within the warm light. When I returned to the present, I was shouting and praising God like the children had done previously. The saints were surrounding me, urging me to "Confess him, confess him!" I had no problem confessing Jesus as Lord. In my spirit, I knew I had just passed from a world of darkness into a world of light, and the light was Jesus Christ. I have encountered numerous tests, trials and tribulations since that day but I have never doubted my salvation.

The spiritual birth of individual believers can be as unique and different as we are as a diversified group of people. Only the Father, the Son and the Holy Spirit know exactly what happens during the transitional phase of being born again. This process is the beginning of a whole new life for every believer. Sometimes newness can mean unfamiliarity. We need to spend some time adjusting to our new lives. We need to know how to live new lives and how to shed old life patterns.

Chapter Two

A NEW CREATION

If anyone is in Christ he has become a new creation, the old nature has gone and a new nature has come (according to 2 Corinthians 5: 17). Having been created anew we are not to regard things from the same point of view we did before we received a new nature. Delivery has actually taken place and spiritual infants were born. We know about worldly knowledge, worldly wisdom and worldly understanding but we may have little or no divine knowledge at this point. We should spend some time becoming familiar with our new Father, our new Savior and our new caretaker, the Holy Spirit. Knowing about our new family members is essential to our spiritual growth and development. Where do we begin? Begin with the Holy Spirit.

At the time of our new birth, we were given the Holy Spirit to dwell within us forever. The mechanism by which he came is hard to explain. He is not someone tangible that we can see with our naked eyes neither can we touch him with our physical hands. We *experience* him instead of *explaining how he came* and seeing his person and touching him with our hands. As flesh gives birth to flesh, the Spirit gives birth to the spirit. As the wind blows wherever it pleases, we hear its sound but cannot tell where it comes from or where it's going. So it is with everyone born of the Spirit (according to John 3: 6, 8). His presence is spiritual and cannot be understood intellectually. He will teach us, guide us to the truth, comfort us and intercede in prayer for us.

We are God's children left in the care of his Spirit for safekeeping. The Spirit himself will testify with our spirit that we are God's children (According to Romans 8: 16-17). Through the Holy Spirit, we can put to death our former deeds as we learn how to live in the newness of life. The actualization of our new birth can assure us of our union with Christ. If we do not have the Spirit of Christ within us, we do not belong to him.   How familiar are you with the Holy Spirit?

The Holy spirit is intelligent and self-conscious with self-determination. He is addressed as God because he is divinity. He proceeds from the Father and the Son but they operate through him. His personality is distinctly different from the Father and the Son, but all three are united in their purpose. Some of his divine attributes include knowledge and sovereignty. He is the same in divine substance and power as the Father and the Son. He was there in the beginning of time when God created man. He was instrumental in the conception of Jesus as a fetus in the womb of Mary. He inspired the prophets and diffused the indwelling Spirit on the day of Pentecost. He was promised to the disciples after Jesus ascended into heaven. He came as the indwelling source of power for believers for the first time in Jerusalem, fifty days after the Passover (or the day of Pentecost). He made a dramatic and powerful, first time appearance. He was heard as the wind, seen as flames of fire and enabled men with little learning to speak in a language that could be understood by those who spoke many different languages. Everyone understood those whom the Spirit dwelled within as if they spoke in their very own language! Needless to say, he will never need to make such an appearance again. Do you believe he is qualified to take care of us?

We, as immature believers, do not have to wait for him to make an entry into our hearts. We do not have to perform any special ritual or use any other means to entice him to come and abide in us. He is a part of the package deal we get with the new birth. God gave him to us when Jesus asked as he promised the disciples he would (according to John 14: 16). *Everyone* who has been born again has the Holy Spirit living in them. Even with the Spirit living within us, we still have the ability to choose or reject his guidance and many of the benefits he wants to share with us. We can still make decisions outside God's will. The Holy Spirit wants to keep us on the right path. However, if we choose to make decisions outside God's will, and we demand to take control of our own will, as much as it grieves him to see us go astray, he will not stop us. He is a gentleman who will not force his way into our affairs. We have to submit to God by surrendering our will before he will intervene in our affairs. God's will cannot be superimposed over our will. We must willingly yield to his way of doing things just as we must willingly receive whatever the Holy Spirit offers us without reservations. Everything he does for us is for our benefit in our new lives.

Always remember, it is God who makes us firm in Christ. He has set his seal of ownership on us, and put *his* Spirit (who is the Holy Spirit) in our heart as a deposit, guaranteeing what is to come (according to 2 Corinthians 1: 22). He *cannot* lie. He is omnipotent. His absolute, unlimited power and authority make him capable of making us firm through Christ. He is omniscient. He knows everything all at once which makes him eternally aware of everything we do. He is omnipresent. His presence is everywhere at all times. No one can go out of his presence at any time. The Psalmist said: Where can I go from your Spirit? Where can I flee from your presence? If I go up to the heavens, you are there; if I make my bed in the depths, you are there. If I rise on the wings of the dawn, if I settle on the far side of the sea, even there your hand will guide me, your right hand will hold me fast (139: 7-10). God watches and directs all our activities at all times when we make Jesus our Lord and follow his directives.

We were all born with unique personalities and traits that

are ours alone. We did not lose any of these traits when our nature was changed. We are to use everything that God blessed us with to bring glory to him. Although we may not yet know what our personal ministries are and how to make godly decisions, we still have the ability to make choices. In the immature stages of life, many of the choices and decisions we make will be consistent with the old nature unless we look to the Holy Spirit for guidance. When we make the confession, "Jesus is Lord," we are actually proclaiming him as Lord and controller of our lives. Lord means one in possession of authority. Jesus already knows that he is Lord. We need to begin to see him as Lord and willingly submit to his authority over every aspect of our lives and supervisor of all of our activities. Our lives are controlled by whomever we put in control of the center (or throne) of our emotions, thoughts and activities. If we are sitting on that throne our lives will be governed by our limitations in knowledge, wisdom and understanding. If Jesus is there all the time, he will direct the Holy Spirit to guide us beside still waters and lead us up pathways of righteousness. Those who continue to live according to the old sinful nature will have their minds set on the things that nature desires. Conversely, those who live according to the Spirit have their minds set on what the Spirit desires. The mind of a sinful man is death, but the mind controlled by the Spirit is life and peace. We, however, are controlled by the Spirit if the spirit of God lives in us (according to Romans 8: 5-9).

The indwelling Holy Spirit and the works he does in the lives of believers are sometimes confused with the gifts of the Spirit. The gifts of the Spirit are administered by the Holy Spirit, but only to believers who are already filled with the Spirit of the Lord. The gifts of the Spirit are *ministering* gifts to be used for the edification of the church or body of believers. *No one believer* will be given *all* the gifts. They are dispersed to individuals to bring about unity as a body. When individual believers use their ministering gifts within the body (the organized church), the gifts can cause the members to come together to form a whole body. That whole body will lack none of the necessary elements used to fulfill the ministries of the church designed and controlled by Jesus. All the gifts of the Spirit glorify God. There are different kinds of gifts, but the same Spirit. There are different kinds of service, but the same Lord. There are different kinds of workings, but the same God works all of them in all men. All these are the works of one and the same Spirit, and he (the Holy Spirit) gives them to each one as he determines (according to 1 Corinthians 12: 4, 11).

We are not to be proud and desire to have the gifts administered to others because they may appear to be greater than our gift. We should graciously receive whatever Spiritual gift the Spirit decides to give us. We should be like clay in the hands of the potter. Will a pot say to the potter; "I do not want to be a pot, it's not important enough, make me a vase?" Does not the potter have the right to make out of the same lump of clay some pottery for noble purposes and some for common use (Romans 9: 21)? One of works of the Holy Spirit is to guide us to the truth as it is, not as we think it should be or someone imagined it was. We should yield and be still when he is working. God has a specific design for each individual believer as each one of us relates to his purpose. Spiritual gifts are used to fulfill his purpose for each of his children as individuals as they interact with the body of believers within the church.

Both natural and spiritual infants must eat to survive. While natural infants crave milk, infant believer's spirits crave the pure sincere milk of the word so that we may grow up in our salvation (according to 1 Peter 2: 2). Natural infant's hunger is unrestrained. Nothing can pacify them except food when they are hungry. We should be that eager to feast upon the word of God. As spiritual infants we must be familiar with the rudiments of the word before we progress to junior food and on to solid food of the word. Unless we are rooted in the elementary things of the word, we will forever go back and forth. We will remain at an infant level of spiritual maturity, failing to thrive in all areas of our new lives. We will be defeated over and over again as we try to fulfill God's purpose. How do we know what the elementary truths are while we are immature and dependent? Everything we need to know is in the word. If we submit to the Holy Spirit, he will gladly teach us in an orderly, congruent manner.

When Jesus called his disciples, before he sent them out into the world, he began to teach them, beginning with the Beatitudes. Every lesson began with *"blessed,"* which was to assure them of spiritual joy because they were partakers of the eternal salvation. These lessons were about an attitude of gratitude and conversion. Spiritual joy was to be upon those who mourned. Their new status would comfort them. Those who became meek and lost worldly pride and arrogance would inherit the earth. *Those who hungered and thirsted after righteousness* were to receive spiritual joy with the assurance of being filled with the word (according to Matthew 5: 4-6).

The elementary truths are things like assurance of salvation and eternal life, the indwelling Holy Spirit, baptism, repentance, faith in God, and eternal judgment. Salvation is a process that begins with the new birth. Believers are saved from the consequences of sin (eternal punishment) and the curse of sin (bondage to Satan). It is made complete when believers take off the robe of the flesh and put on the robe of the Spirit at the end of this mortal life. There is one *major* source of truth, the Holy Bible, unabridged.

We are to be assured of the indwelling Spirit because the word of God says we received him when we received Jesus. Contrary to the teachings of some concerning outward evidence of the Spirit's abode (by someone's pre-set standards), believers are to believe God as he reveals himself in the Word. It is not necessary to prove to anyone at anytime that the Spirit of God dwells within us. Remember, our new birth is personal, unique and between each believer and the Lord. The Spirit's power within us will be made manifest by our behavior and our works. All we do should be to please God *first*. Everyone and everything else should become secondary. Make a tree good and it's fruits will be good, make a tree bad and it's fruits will be bad, for a tree is recognized by its fruit (according to Matthew 12: 33).

Water baptism has no saving power within its self. It should be done as an act of obedience and as a symbol of identifying with the death burial and resurrection of Jesus Christ. We are immersed in water to portray our death to sin and brought up out of the water to portray our new nature enabling us to live new lives (according to Romans 6: 4). Baptism should always follow (and not precede) the new birth. Jesus submitted to water baptism, setting an example for us to follow. He commanded his followers, past, present and future to baptize new disciples in the name of the Father, the Son and the Holy Spirit (according to Matthew 28: 19). Faith in God is intimately involved in everything believers do. Faith is believing in God's ability, willingness and integrity to perform the things he promises in his word. Our belief system should be devoted to God first and what he says in the word. It was through faith that our new birth came to pass. Believe the Scriptures as the God-breathed word as the Holy Spirit inspired writers to document all the things pertaining to our new lives. The entire life and growth of all believers is based on their faith in God and his word. Each believer has been given a measure of faith. We do not need a lot of faith to do what we have been assigned to do in life. We just need to act on whatever amount of faith we have. Our faith will increase as we grow in the knowledge of the Lord.

There are many believers who do not believe that the eternal judgment means an eternity in hell. Understanding of who God is and how pure and powerful he is may motivate believers to attest to his righteousness in judgment. God is just in all his means of judging. Some of his chosen people were so wicked in their deeds until he judged them before the end of time. The Israelites were judged for failure to believe in the promise of God. After being led out of bondage in Egypt and witnessing the parting of the red sea, they did not believe God had given them the land of Caanan as he promised. All the adults among them died in the wilderness without entering into God's rest. The inhabitants of Sodom and Gomorrah were judged because of their sexual immorality and perverted sexual practices. The cities and all their inhabitants were burned with brimstone and made desolate. These cities were examples of the eternal judgment to be suffered by those who commit similar deeds. They will be burned by eternal fire (according to Jude 5-7). The eternal judgment is real just as hell is real. Anyone who rejects the Son of the living God will be judged and punished along with Satan and the false prophets. They will all be thrown into the lake of burning fire and tormented day and night for ever and ever (according to Revelation 20: 10).

We have already expressed a desire to repent and chose to live a life differently from our former lives but we still need to express godly sorrow for misdeeds along the way. We are not to repent for deeds we have already been forgiven of and we do not have the power to change our lives without directives from the Father. Repent means to turn from the road we are traveling, and head in a different direction. For infant believers, that is a work in progress. Once we have become established in the rudimentary truths and have fully digested them, we are ready to move forward. We can begin to find out what we are supposed to do next and how to begin to walk in a different direction.

Chapter Three

ADJUSTING TO A NEW LIFE

Now we know who we are and are assured of our new status and new nature we are held accountable for our ungodly actions. Whatever seeds we plant along the way will grow up into a harvest. We will always reap the harvest of whatever we sow. Before we begin to sow in this new life we should review the life of the forerunner of Jesus and even Jesus himself during their formative years. Our new lives should be adjusted to specific standards set forth in the word of God. These two anointed examples followed those standards.

John, the forerunner for Jesus was sanctified from the time of his conception. His parents knew what his ministry would be before he was born. They, no doubt, told him he was to go before Jesus with the message of repentance. Before he began to minister, John denied himself of the delicacies of life in food and communication with others. He isolated himself and went into the wilderness for a season. He ate such things as the earth produced like wild honey and berries. When the fullness of time had come, he presented himself publicly and began his ministry.

Jesus, who was God incarnate, was always sinless, sanctified and completely pure. He spent his formative years as a carpenter's son as he grew in wisdom and stature. He remained obedient to his earthly parents until his time came to fulfill his duties in the flesh. He submitted to water baptism and waited until the fullness of time had come for him to begin his earthly ministry. We are to adjust to our new lives by denial of self, growing strong in wisdom and waiting on the Lord for direction. While we are adjusting, we need to know what we are to adjust to. This will come through divine knowledge, divine wisdom and divine understanding. How will we come by these important components at this phase of our new lives?

God, who knows everything, is everywhere all the time. He has all power and is concerned about all our individual needs, no matter how insignificant they may seem. Before he will work on our behalf, we must agree with him that we have needs beyond our ability to satisfy. While we can find everything we will ever need to know in the Bible, we will need help in interpreting what it all means, and how to apply the principles to our daily lives. We can communicate all our needs to God in prayer. At this point, we should learn how to pray effectively. This means to be in a position of righteousness so that we may be heard and answered. Believers can always look to Jesus as an example.

Every time Jesus prayed he was effective. He always prayed with assurance without wondering if his Father heard him or intended to answer him. He simply said; "I will pray to the Father and he will......." He was always in the will of the Father because he was always faithful and obedient with the right attitude. We can pray with assurance too, as long as we meet the standards set forth in the word. Prayer is the highest form of communication between man and God. It is always initiated by man but sometimes prompted by the Spirit. When we approach the throne of God we want his attention so we may talk with him and have him listen to us. We should also wait for him to talk to us while we listen to his directives. God is gracious in that he permits us to come before his throne with confidence so that we may obtain mercy and help in our time of need (according to Hebrews 4: 16). Remember though, God's eyes are too pure to look on sin and he will not tolerate unrighteousness. Some of the major conditions we must meet to approach his throne are:

faith, forgiveness, and submissiveness which will lead to right-eousness. Since all power over heaven and earth is in the hands of Jesus, all prayers must be prayed in Jesus' name.

Faith is being sure of what we hope for and certain we will receive what we desire even though we cannot see how (accord-ing to Hebrews 11: 1). Our confidence or faith should be in the power, integrity and faithfulness of God. Unless we believe God can and will make good on his promises, our prayers are futile. Doubt is the opposite of faith. We doubt when our hope is not rooted in the reality of the promises. Our faith should not be in mortals or unfounded doctrines. We have but to search the Scriptures to see the testimonies of the prophets of old and see faith in action when we doubt God's promises. When we have total confidence in the Lord we can ask him anything, no mat-ter how impossible it may seem. If we have enough confi-dence in God to believe that he is not confined to circumstances and situations we will learn to pray above and beyond our own circumstances and situations.

It seemed impossible for Abraham and Sarah to conceive a child, given their circumstances. Both were far, far beyond the childbearing age when God promised Abraham he would become the father of many nations. Abraham *knew* God. He was certain that God, who could call things into existence that never existed before, could do anything. He didn't look at his circumstances neither did he ever think it was impossible for God to do what he said he would do. He did not waver at the promise through unbelief. He was *fully persuaded* that God was able to do as he had promised. He was strengthened in faith and gave glory to God (according to Romans 4: 17-21). We can be as con-fident as Abraham was. I was involved in a seemingly, impos-sible situation that tested my faith over ten years ago. We are never sure how much faith we have until it's tested.

My god-daughter was within a few weeks of graduation from UCLA. The five years she spent there had been hard for her in numerous ways. She had met with her counselor at the beginning of her last year and several times in between. One day she received a message from her counselor that she had miscalculated her credits. She needed another specific course before she would be able to graduate. It was too late to pick up another class. She telephoned me from the campus in total distress. Through sobs, she told me of her dilemma, assuring me she could not spend another year there. Trying to sound calm and reassuring, I suggested we give the problem to the Lord and he would work out this situation to her advantage. We often prayed together so she came right over and we began to search the Scriptures for something to hang on to. We were guided to Abraham and his seemingly impossible situation. We began to pray without trying to figure out how God was going to work but with assurance that he was able to work in this situation. Before we began to pray we examined our lives and adjusted them to fit the standards required by God.

We asked the Holy Spirit to bring all unconfessed sins to our memory so we could forgive and be forgiven. We surrendered our will to God and asked that his will prevail. We denied ourselves of any delicacies and drank water and juice while we fasted. We isolated ourselves from anything ungodly and anyone distracting. We went before the throne of God and made our petition known to him. We prayed the problem and left the solution up to him. We told him what our desires were but admitted our will was imperfect, then we waited. While we were waiting we prayed and sang spiritual songs and read the word. The Lord didn't answer us all at once. He directed us along the way. My god-daughter was told she would need an appointment with the chancellor. She was informed no one had ever petitioned for graduation under her circumstances before and she was going to be unsuccessful in her attempt. The chancellor was booked up until after graduation. We hoped against hope and prayed specifically for an appointment with the chancellor. After what seemed like an eternity, she was granted an appointment with the chancellor, to the amazement of the counselor. She had done some work with a professor earlier in the year. She was able to use that work as course credit and graduate with her class without returning to make-up class work. When we meet God's standards he will readily hear and answer us. At first my god-daughter was angry with her counselor. Before we began to petition the Lord she had to rid herself of the anger and forgive her counselor for the error. It may have been a part of God's plan to test her faith.

Forgiveness is a two-fold experience that is essential to effective prayers. The lip service of saying "I'm sorry," cannot complete the process of forgiving or being forgiven unless it's accompanied by a godly decision within the heart. We must forgive others of their sins against us before we will be forgiven for ours against the Lord (according to Matthew 6: 15). Failure to properly forgive is a major deterrent to the hearing of many prayers. If we don't forgive others, just as our Father forgives us, we will not be forgiven of him. We cannot go before his throne as long as we are in a state of sinfulness. If we cherish sin within our hearts, the Lord will not hear us (according to Psalm 16: 18). To develop a forgiving spirit, we must clothe ourselves in compassion, kindness, gentleness and patience as the chosen people of God. Bear with each other and forgive whatever grievances we may have against each other and forgive others in the same manner as the Lord forgives us (according to Colossians 3: 13). The Lord shows us how he forgives in I John 1: 9. If we acknowledge our sins as sin, calling them by name, he is trustworthy, faithful and ready to forgive us. When he forgives us, he purifies us from the wickedness and evils that come with sin and then bring us back into his favor as if the sin never happened. He blots out our transgressions for his sake and remembers our sins no more. If we put away the sin in our hand, he will allow no evil to dwell in our homes (according to Job 11: 14). Sin separates us from the ability to fellowship with the Lord. The only thing he wants to hear from us is "forgive me," when we have a spirit of forgiveness in our hearts.

This is exactly how we should forgive others. We should release our transgressors from the guilt associated with sin and blot the sin out of our minds. Restore them to the place they had with us before they sinned against us and treat them as if the sin never occurred. Do not bring the transgression up in conversation or discuss it with anyone ever again. How the transgressor responds should not effect our forgiveness. Everyone will be required to account for his own response. If we respond in an ungodly manner in any situation, we need to seek forgiveness, even if we think we are the injured party. I learned this lesson the hard way.

As director of the Young Adults at church, I had formed a special bond with the group as they had with me. We were growing in the word by leaps and bounds when the pastor announced from the pulpit one Sunday that he had appointed a new director for the Young Adults. I had no prior notifications neither was I aware of any problems with the group. I was down right mad and used every available opportunity to sound off about it. I fumed for a few weeks and thought under the circumstances I should leave the church. We were readily approaching the day for the Lord's Supper to be served. I was out of sorts spiritually and prayed for guidance from the Holy Spirit. When I asked that my sins be brought before me so that I could confess them, the Spirit directed me to ask the pastor for forgiveness! I really thought he should have asked me for forgiveness but I realized that my intellect was limited with reference to the Spirit. I called and asked for forgiveness for my wrong response and all the misdeeds that followed. I felt immediate relief and peace flooded my being. All that fuming and disarray because I did not forgive so that I could be forgiven had harmed me probably more than the transgressor. When we submit to the Lord in sincerity, he will point out the areas of sin in our lives.

Forgiveness leads to righteousness. The Lord purifies us and we are holy vessels privileged to enter into his presence in prayer. Submission is inclusive with regard to righteousness. We can only be pure and righteous in a state of submissiveness. Some of us take pride in our ability to make informed, intelligent decisions. We cling fast to our imperfect, limited will and live on the fringes of the life appointed to us. Once it becomes life to us that our intellect is so far below the intellect of God until it is seen as ignorance, we can willingly submit to God and give up our will and be controlled by the highest power there is. Our will does not always conform to God's will so we should stop struggling, complaining and murmuring and humble ourselves under the mighty hand of God. We should be relieved to know that we can cast all our cares and anxieties upon him because he cares for us. Admit that we are not sufficient in ourselves to claim anything for ourselves. All our sufficiency comes from the Lord (according to 2 Corinthians 3: 5). The Lord wants us to be dependent upon him for everything.

Jesus was totally dependent upon his Father. He said; "I came down from heaven, not to do my will, but the will of him that sent me" (according to John 6: 38). He was not attempting to bring gratification or glory to himself, but seeking only to please the Father. He admitted that he did nothing of himself, but only what the Father told him. We are like branches who receive life from Jesus, who is the vine. Apart from him we *can* do nothing. Once we rid ourselves of our imperfect will we will see life differently and desire to do the will of the Father.

Surrendering and submitting is not a one time process but something we must do continuously so that we may freely communicate with God and hear him when he responds to us. Yielding the right of way to the Lord will bring us to a state of separation from the things that displease him. We can approach him honestly, virtuously and correctly with clean hearts. We will be able to humble ourselves unselfishly with renewed, transformed minds as we pray for our needs to be met without thinking about worldly things. The fervent prayer of a righteous man is powerful and effective (according to James 5: 6). Faith, forgiveness and submission are steps towards righteousness. Although God's eyes are on the righteous and his ears are attentive to their prayers, all prayers must be prayed in the name of Jesus before we receive a response. Not just a name attached to the end of a prayer, but praying in Jesus' name with the understanding that power emits from the name. Recognizing, always, that it was Jesus who made forgiveness possible and who gave us the privilege to pray. God gave him all power over us. We are to always acknowledge him in an attitude of reverence and gratitude when we pray.

As we make some of the necessary adjustments and begin to conform to them, we are ready to move to another level of spiritual development. All spiritual children do not grow at the same pace. The order that God plans for the development for each of his children may not be the same, but we will all learn the same truths even if we learn them in different ways, if we follow the teachings of the Holy Spirit. Even when we learn how to communicate with the Lord, there is still much to know about living the life of a true believer. When we apply what we learn we will grow from spiritual infants to spiritual toddlers in Christ. Spiritual toddlers are trained differently from spiritual infants. Their lessons become a bit more accelerated.

Chapter Four

TRAIN UP THE CHILD

We are now like natural toddlers just learning how to walk. As we learn to walk in the newness of life, our gait may be a bit unsteady and we may not always arrive in the exact spot we aimed for. We may stagger a bit at some of the promises and stumble at the word while we are learning how to walk in the spirit. We may even fall more than a few times but if we keep practicing we will become better and better. Our gait will become more steady we will walk and not become weary and land in the very spot for which we were aiming. While we are unsteady on our feet though, we need someone to pick us up when we fall, nurse our bruises and set us back on the right path. We should not just follow anybody who seems okay. We should pray and ask the Spirit to direct us to a local church were we may be assisted by *practicing* believers with spiritual experience and maturity. Pray also for a leader who preaches and teaches from the word of God unabridged. Watered down versions of the truth may delete the very facts we need for proper development at this stage of growth. Be as certain as you can that the leader you select leads by precept and example, just as Jesus did.

Your needs may be met in your present church and the Spirit may lead you to stay where you are. Wherever you go and whatever you do, follow the example of the Bereans in Acts 17: 11. They received the messages of Paul with great eagerness but searched the Scriptures daily to see if what Paul said was true.

The Lord promised to give his people shepherds after his own heart, who would lead them with knowledge and understanding (according to Jeremiah 3: 15). Shepherds appointed by the Holy Spirit are charged with keeping watch over all the flock that they were called to overseer (according to Acts 20: 28). Unfortunately we *must* be alert as we seek a place to worship, fellowship and serve. There are self-appointed shepherds, evangelist, teachers and prophets in the world today in growing numbers. The Scripture warned us that there would be false prophets and teachers among us who would secretly introduce personal opinions and teachings that cause moral and spiritual destruction to those who accept them as true. They are motivated by greed and make a business out of the Christian faith to satisfy their own selfish egos. They will exploit their followers with stories they made up themselves (according to 2 Peter 2: 1-2).

Toddling believers are fragile and do not need to be put in such precarious positions at this stage of development. That's why it is of paramount importance that we pray and wait on the Holy Spirit to lead us to a place of worship of his choosing. If the teachings are different from the gospel found in the Holy Bible, do not linger, leave as quickly and as quietly as possible. Some may think spiritual toddlers cannot digest all this just yet, but the Holy Spirit is there for guidance if we listen to him. If we compare the mission of the local church with the purpose for establishing local churches we may get an idea about the church's leadership practices right away. We should not hesitate to ask about the mission statement of the church and how the church fulfills the overall anointed mission of the church established with Jesus Christ as the head. The mission of all local churches is:

To fulfill the divine commission: Go and make disciples of all nations, baptizing them in the name of the Father and of the Son and of the Holy Spirit and teaching them to obey everything I have commanded you. And surely I am with you always to the very end of the age (according to Jesus in Matthew 28: 19-20)

To witness for Christ: You will receive power when the Holy Spirit comes on you; you will be my witness in all Jerusalem, in all Judea and Samaria, and to the ends of the earth (Acts 1: 8). That is equivalent to home, within the body, the surrounding communities, outer neighborhoods, then other cities, states and countries, in that order.

To impart spiritual knowledge: Many peoples will come and say, come, let us go to the house of the God of Jacob. He will teach us his ways, so that we may walk in his paths (Micah 4:2).

Those are some of the major reasons for establishing local churches. The most profound business of the church is to make and train disciples so that the gospel can go forth. In keeping with Jesus' example, disciples are pupils of the word before they can become doers and carriers of the word. God ordained leaders are responsible for teaching the word of God unabridged.

Ignorance of the word is no excuse for believers who are developing skills in their new lives. No one has to remain ignorant. We can begin to read and study the Bible for ourselves. If we cannot read, pray more fervently for divine guidance. Just reading the Bible is different from studying it. Reading involves acquiring knowledge from the printed word without in-depth research. As part of my daily devotions, I read from the Psalm. Studying is reading from books of the Bible or specific passages of Scripture and researching the passages verse by verse. Scripture is interpreted by Scripture but it takes time to grasp the complete understanding of one verse when we are studying. To study effectively, we need a Bible with a concordance; which is an alphabetical index with all or most of the major words within the Bible. A Bible Commentary; which is a book that explains and illustrates the books of the Bible. Look for one that gives background information that is invaluable to the study of the Bible. The background information explains why, when, where and other important specifics about each book. This information can drastically change the way some epistles should be viewed. Invest in a Bible dictionary that defines words from a spiritual perspective.

Develop a time, a place and a plan for studying the Bible. Put forth every effort to study at regular pre-planned intervals. Join a good Bible Study group that lends itself to questions and discussions. Try to read the Bible every day. If you are not sure where to start, begin with one of the four gospels. The book of John is a very good starting place. If you want to know more about specifics, look up the word that interests you in the concordance or the Bible dictionary. Read all the passages of Scripture associated with that word. This should give you a working knowledge of any subject that interest you. Always pray for the Holy Spirit to assist you during each Bible study session. If you do not seem to retain what you read at first, do not become anxious. The Holy Spirit is with you. He will teach you and bring all things to our remembrance that Jesus said in the word, after you have read it (according to John 16: 26).

We study the Bible to acquire knowledge about God, his promises, his will and how it all relates to us. Knowledge is merely an acquisition of information. It must be seasoned with divine wisdom before we can use it to bring glory to God. The adversary knows the Bible well but he does not have the anointing. He knows that the Scriptures will tell us about him and his tactics as well as our ability to resist him. He does not want us to know any of this. With divine knowledge and wisdom, we need divine understanding before we can take the words from the pages of the Bible and apply them to our daily lives. The more we read and study the word the more knowledge we acquire. We must pray and ask God to give us divine wisdom.

Wisdom consists of a collection of life experiences, applications of knowledge and how we respond to the things that happen to us in life. It involves the practical application of knowledge. Anyone who lacks wisdom should ask God, who gives generously to all without finding fault, and it will be given to him. When he asks he must believe and not doubt because he who doubts will be like a wave of the sea, blown and tossed by the sea. He will not receive anything of the Lord because he is unstable in all his ways (according to James 1: 5-8). Divine wisdom does not conform to secular rationalizations. Spiritual truths are expressed in spiritual words, taught by the Spirit. Anyone without the Spirit cannot accept the things that come from the Spirit because they are spiritually discerned. The Spirit does not speak to our intellect, he speaks to our spirit and we understand him by the Spirit.

Wisdom teaches us how to process knowledge and how to examine the life experiences that come our way. God is aware of every test, every life experience and every trial that come into our lives. He either sends most of them or permits the enemy to send them. He does not arbitrarily send or permit things to happen to us. Each life experience has a defined purpose and is part of a larger plan. Once we understand the significance of each life experience we are able to respond properly. Until we learn the proposed lesson, the experience will not disappear, and we will not be promoted to the next phase of development. We can develop failure to thrive syndrome at any stage of growth by failing to examine each experience sent our way. The same incident may take on different forms. The Lord works with us until we finally get it. He really wants us to grow up. Some growth experiences may come in the form of painful trials or tests. Others may come as special, unexpected opportunities or blessings. We can only process, apply and respond to experiences we understand. Jesus opened the minds of his disciples so they could understand spiritual principles. I believe he will do the same thing for us if we ask him.

To understand is to thoroughly know the nature and significance of what the Scripture or even an experience means to us individually. Sometimes we can visualize, with our spiritual eyes, the spiritual truths presented to us and explain to ourselves and others (or interpret), the concept. Without divine understanding we are likely to make mistakes in our judgment of things. God is patient and long-suffering with us. He will not cast us off when we stumble unintentionally.

Through understanding, we gain wisdom and knowledge, and by responding and applying knowledge we are made wiser. The final outcome will give us unforgettable testimonies and increase our faith. Knowledge, wisdom and understanding are an inseparable trio working hand-in-hand to train new believers up in the way we should go.

Understanding, like everything else believers need, comes from God. It is the Spirit in us, the breath of the almighty that gives us understanding (according to Job 32: 8). His understanding is limitless. If we want our daily pathways to be made straight, we must trust in the Lord with all our emotions, minds and souls without allowing our limited understanding to get in the way. By inviting his presence to overshadow everything we do, say or think, we can be assured of his constant guidance. If we turn towards wisdom from him, and listen for him to speak wise interpretations to our hearts, and apply his directives to every life experience, we will grow in grace. If we cry out for insight, cry aloud for understanding and look diligently for it like we are searching for hidden treasures or precious metals, we will understand the fear of the Lord and find the knowledge of God. The Lord gives wisdom and from his mouth comes knowledge and understanding (according to Proverbs 2: 2-6).

Anointed knowledge, divine wisdom and understanding are the doors every believer must walk through continuously if they are to become followers of Jesus Christ. Like the caterpillar that spends time wandering around in the soil, the trees and other vegetation before she hibernates in her cocoon, so are we. After a season she comes forth as a lovely butterfly with breathtakingly, colorful wings. She now soars high above her former status spreading beauty wherever she goes. Believers preparing to sit at the feet of Jesus and learn how to follow him, wander around in the word of God as spiritual toddlers. Then we become more mature in the word as we separate ourselves from the world and spend time in a cocoon praying, studying and examining life experiences. Before long we will emerge as bright and beautiful as butterflies, soaring on the wings of eagles in our spirits as we endeavor to follow Jesus' examples.

Following Jesus' baptism he was led by the Spirit in the desert to be tempted by the devil. We can expect to be tempted by the devil as well. God will not let us be tempted beyond our ability to resist. Each time the devil approached Jesus he used the Scriptures to rebuke the devil saying; "It is written..." We are to do like wise. We do not have power, apart from the Holy Spirit, to rebuke the devil. We are to use the power of the word of God against the enemy of God.

If we want God's blessings along the way and the opportunity to see him someday, we must remain pure through and through. Jesus wanted disciples past, present and future to understand that following him involved making some changes in attitudes, lifestyles and habits. The finished product is what Jesus wants us to see. Before changes can be fully realized we must be shaped and molded as the old is taken away so the new can shine through. For believers, this is done by tests or examinations, trials, persecutions and temptations.

Chapter Five

MAKING MOLDING AND MATURING

Examinations or tests, trials and persecutions are extremely vital to spiritual growth and development. As we come to the end of one developmental level of growth we are tested and tried before being promoted to the next level. Tests, their accompanying afflictions and distressing experiences, can devastate growing believers. We often think we are home free after we have been born anew and the discomforts caused by the trials are not God ordained. Immature believers need to understand why trials come and how to endure the hardships caused by them, so that they can be easier to endure.

Tests and examinations are instruments of spiritual molding and shaping as the Lord measures our growth. Each experience is a process aimed at spiritual maturity. Although many of our examinations can be painful, they are necessary. The process is as tedious and precise as the shaping of diamonds when they are in the process of being made perfect. Trials are like the pressure applied as the instruments of molding are used. They are accompanied by distress and discomfort that we suffer when we are afflicted in any way. Sometimes the afflictions can become extremely painful, distressing and almost unbearable. These are called tribulations. However, none will ever be as great as the agony Jesus suffered on his way to the cross and no distress will ever surpass the moment when the

Father turned his face from Jesus. Throughout our growth and development, whatever we are faced with, the Holy Spirit will be available to help us if we call out to him.

Testing is one of God's ways of purifying us so that we may share in Christ's glory. However, we must share in his sufferings before we are capable of sharing in his glory. He sees us as diamonds in the rough. He will take us through phases of molding, shaping and restructuring so that our true illumination can be seen. He planned our salvation before the world was formed, from our new birth throughout eternity. He sees what we are capable of becoming.

Diamonds are precious stones found in the soil of the earth. They are covered with dirt and debris when they are extracted from the earth. They must be washed thoroughly before being handed over to the specialist who will make them useful things of beauty. Before the Father drew us to his Son, we were encrusted with the filth of the world. God sent his word out to extract us. When the word of God goes out from his mouth, it will not return to him empty. God's word will accomplish what he desires and achieve the purpose for which he sent it (according to Isaiah 55: 11). After the word extracted us from the dirt we were washed in the blood of Jesus to cleanse us from all the stains of sin. Diamond masses are taken to a specialist who will cut them, mold them and shape them to be set in a setting of the owner's choosing. We are entrusted into the care of the Holy Spirit and our owner, the Father, who tells him how to make and mold us for our final setting which is eternal life. Shaping of diamonds is done with precision tools, patience and in a progressive manner. They must be chiseled with minute details. Only small particles can be cut at each setting. Some areas are chiseled and others are shaved. Flawless diamonds must not be cracked or cut in ways that would decrease their value. The Lord is precise, patient and progressive as he makes us flawless instruments of beauty. Until we are shaped after the will of God, we remain like invaluable masses with no control, no direction and no discipline. The diamond endures the tedious process necessary for it to become perfect for its chosen setting. The owner inspects it for color, clarity and carats when it's completed. Its beauty can truly be appreciated as the brilliant whites, red-oranges, blues and greens sparkle when they hit the polyhedral angles when it comes in contact with light. A fine stone is ready to be set. The Holy Spirit is actively involved in the tedious process of making and molding us according to the Father's specifications. Sometimes we struggle, grumble and complain while the Spirit is working with us but he is patient. He waits on us to be still and yield to the Master's will before moving ahead with the process of making and molding. We are not ready for the final inspection yet. We still have more to learn and many more examinations to pass. The process will be painful sometimes as the Spirit chisel, file and shave away unnecessary portions of our lives.

Being still is one of the things young believers have not yet mastered. We are excited about our growth and want to be everywhere, doing everything at once. When we are being tested for perseverance, we must surrender our will and be still long enough for perseverance to finish her work of making us mature, lacking nothing (according to James 1:2-4). If we remain steadfast, keep the faith and endure the discomforts of the trials without faltering, we will be blessed. The desire to become flawless and please the Lord should sustain us. One of the best ways to remain steadfast in the midst of trials is to praise the Lord continuously and focus on the crown of life that the Lord has promised to those who love him. Be assured and reassured that we will not be tried or tested beyond our ability to endure without faltering. God knows how much each of us can bear at every level of growth. Remember, each trial has significant value and that God does not operate on impulse. For a little while, we may suffer grief due to the many types of trials we will encounter. However, they must come to prove our faith genuine and will result in honor, praise and glory when Jesus is revealed. Our faith is more precious than gold refined by fire, which will perish (according to 1 Peter 1: 6, 7).

The divine wisdom from God will enable us to face afflictions with practical, divine insight. The Spirit will always be there to take us safely through the discomfort, pain and distress. Sometimes we get anxious and begin to look everywhere else except to the Lord for comfort, support and advice. If we call out to him he will comfort us. We usually do not think we can just wait until the storm passes. We think we should be doing something or we are being punished for something. In frustration, we frantically ask the Lord to tell us what we should be doing. We think we have missed the message if he does not say anything. Often his silence is the *message*. If he does not say anything it's probably because he does not want us to do anything but wait. We can be of good cheer while we are waiting and rejoice in hope. Not because of the trials themselves, but because we know that God will see us through them and elevate us to another level of maturity. Think about other trials and how the Lord enabled us to endure them and the testimony and blessedness we received after we endured them. Every test *seems* to be the *hardest test we have ever encountered.* Trust in the Lord's willingness and ability to handle the present situation in a way that creates growth and glorifies him. As long as we are certain that we are in his will we can rest in his sovereignty to do what pleases him without harming us. We belong to the Father, he will not permit us to be handled too roughly as long as we abide in him and his word abides in us.

Our level of maturity is determined by how we respond to trials brought about because of examinations. It's very easy to put all our trust in the Lord in times of peace and blessedness. We can *speak* of a good righteous walk with the Lord during such times. But when the actual journey begins and we leave the *still water sides* and begin to climb up the rough sides of the mountain, true faithfulness, steadfastness and spiritual insight will be revealed. However, we should know that God has always tried the people he loved. Everyone did not always respond in the same manner, just as all of us will respond in different manners. Everyone was rewarded or judged according to the way they responded. Sometimes the adversary was permitted to enter into the affairs of God's people to see if their faith was genuine. God may permit the adversary to enter into our affairs for the same purpose.

Job was very wealthy and considered righteous and upright by the Lord. The Lord suggested to the adversary that he tempt Job. The Lord defined the terms under which Job was to be tempted. The adversary afflicted his entire body with painful sores. He suffered loss of all his earthly possessions, his family and his good health. He grumbled and complained when his friends insisted he must have done something wrong to cause such afflictions but he remained faithful and steadfast. He refused to deny God or curse God and die to flee from his afflictions. Instead of cursing God, he said; "I know my redeemer lives." He understood that he was being tried but he did not know why, yet he said with assurance; "When I am tried I will come through as pure gold." He was very familiar with God. After Job endured the afflictions the Lord restored everything he had lost, multi-fold. Paul was buffered with a physical affliction by a messenger of Satan and sought the Lord three times for healing. Paul was not healed but he was assured that the Lord's grace was sufficient enough to sustain him. Paul found a reason to rejoice in his weakness. His response pleased the Lord. Abraham was required to sacrifice the son he had waited years to conceive. He did not think the Lord was taxing him too heavily. He obediently took Isaac to the altar of sacrifice, believing that even if Isaac had to be killed the Lord could raise him up again. His response pleased the Lord and another sacrifice was provided in Isaac's stead. Suffering and believing go hand-in-hand. We should view suffering and trials permitted or sent by the Lord as a privilege granted to the children of God to make and mold us after his will. For it has been granted you on behalf of Christ not only to believe on him but also to suffer for him (according to Phillipians 1: 29). Everyone born of God will be tested and suffer trials. If we are indeed God's children and expect to share in the glory of Christ Jesus, we are appointed to share in his sufferings (according to Romans 8: 17).

Suffering produces perseverance, perseverance produces character and character produces hope. Hope does not disappoint us because God has poured out his love into our hearts by the Holy Spirit whom he has given us (according to Romans 5: 4, 5). The Lord sends rays of sunshine and new, fresh hope to us after we overcome the testing of our faith. We gain first hand knowledge of how the Lord works on behalf of his children. We can testify to his grace and mercy personally. We should use these testimonies to assure other believers that nothing strange is happening to them when they encounter trials. Trails do not necessarily mean we are not in God's will. Sometimes they come because we are in God's will and God is ready to move us to another level of maturity. Until we are ready for our final setting in eternity, the shaping of our lives will continue. They will not become easier. The more we grow the more difficult our examinations will become. We are expected to learn how to better respond to each new trial. When we respond in ways that please God we will be blessed in accordance with our responses. If we respond negatively, we will be tested with the same trial until we learn how to respond in a godly manner. If we look at tests, examinations and persecution as challenges and strive to overcome them with our spiritual lives intact, we can endure them even when we think we are not strong enough. Some of these challenges may motivate us to use all our spiritual energy and spiritual resources but God made all these resources available to us to be used in such times. God will fill us up when we think we are becoming empty and cannot function.

Just when I thought I could rest for a season, about ten years ago, I was challenged with a virulent, life threatening catastrophe. I am a Registered Nurse by profession and was working in a teaching hospital. One day I felt a sharp pain in my right eye as I worked at my desk. I went to the eye clinic for an eye examination, thinking I only needed a new prescription. That was the beginning of a three month journey through what seemed like hell to me. The ophthalmologist told me I had a very serious condition; perhaps early signs of multiple sclerosis or maybe even a brain tumor. He suggested I see a private clinician immediately. I went into denial and dismissed his diagnoses as premature. My vision began to change rapidly in my right eye after that examination. I began to search for a private ophthalmologist to identify the cause of the rapidly diminishing vision. The resident who saw me originally had completed his training and left before I had an opportunity to get a referral from him. I began to pray and search the Scriptures for comfort and direction. The Spirit kept leading me to passages on trials and suffering. I became angry with the Lord and cried out; "I know about suffering, I am in trouble and I need your help now." My anger was short lived because there was no hope in anything else but the Lord for me. After I had seen more ophthalmologists than I care to remember and received a wide range of answers from each of them, I surrendered my all to the Lord. I was told that my problem was due to the aging process by one doctor. I may have accepted that if the problem had been in both eyes. Another doctor told me I needed to see a psychiatrist because the problem was all in my head. I began to learn how to suffer and remain in God's will through all the lessons the Lord was sending my way. I became calmer and began to deal with some of the things that confronted me. The Lord began to deal with me spiritually but this did not make the problem any less traumatic. My faith was being tested to the limits.

One day, during this phase of testing, I was driving on the freeway when suddenly my world just went black. My knees began to shake and my heart began to pound within my chest at an extremely rapid pace. I was more afraid than I have ever been in my life. I called out; "Lord please help me!" My vision returned as quickly as it vanished. I was safe and had not harmed anyone else. I was so grateful to the Lord until I began to cry and praise him for his presence in my time of distress. I began to search for answers and direction more fervently.

Almost three months passed and I was no closer to a diagnosis than I was when the problem first presented itself. I was beginning to grow tired and weary. The adversary used every opportunity to needle me, often waking me from a sound sleep and telling me; "You are going to die or be a vegetable for the remainder of your life." I prayed and prayed for the Lord to heal me without any mortal intervention all along the way. He had healed me of an incurable disease ten years prior to the onset of this problem. I knew he was able to do it again if he so desired. I even went to a "healing service," hoping against hope to be made whole again. My faith was stable and I knew I was in God's will but the Lord chose to exercise his sovereignty and intervene in other ways. I did not tell anyone what I was going through. I went to work every day, I continued to teach classes at church and do many of the things I normally did. I isolated myself as much as possible, fasted, prayed and continued to search the Scriptures for comfort.

I began to think, "If only I could get a referral to the Jules Stein Eye Center at UCLA, I would at least find someone to diagnose my problem." I think the Spirit was directing me. One Sunday night as I was praying, I asked the Lord to permit me to get a referral to UCLA on the following day. That Monday at work, as I talked with a spiritual sister in the hallway, the Spirit urged me to tell her about my dilemma. I was obedient and help was on the way. She was the secretary to the Chief of Ophthalmology who also saw patients at Jules Stein. She told him about me and he made arrangements to see me at UCLA within two days. He did not diagnose my problem but he sent me to a specialist who ordered a diagnostic scan of my brain. I had a rather large brain tumor wrapped around the main artery supplying blood to the brain. The tumor was encroaching on the optic nerve (the nerve that controls the eyes) on the right side and had to be surgically removed rather quickly. When I asked, "What Lord, what shall I do?" He assured me I was to be a testimony for him following the outcome of the surgery.

I was confident in the Lord's ability to do what was best for me. I was beyond caring about life or death. I just did not want to be a vegetable and become a burden on anyone. I asked the Lord for a Christian surgeon. The original surgeon scheduled to operate on me, whom I had never met, broke his leg and was replaced. The replacement surgeon assured me he had been born again. I went to James 5: 14, 15 in the Bible that says; Is any of you sick? He should call the elders of the church to pray over him and anoint him with oil in the name of the Lord and the prayer offered in faith will make the sick person well. I asked the Lord to make me whole or take me home. I had come to know that we do not always hear *all* the Lord is telling us when we are in the midst of our own crises. As I read that passage of Scripture and began to meditate upon it, a passage from Isiah 55: 8, 9 kept coming to mind. "For my thoughts are not your thoughts, neither are your ways my ways. As the heavens are higher than the earth, so are my ways higher than your ways and my thoughts than your thoughts," said the Lord. I just put everything into his hands and said; "Handle it Lord." The night before I was scheduled to be admitted to the hospital I asked the Lord to speak to me and give me some assurance. He was silent. I had already requested prayer of the pastor as the Scripture had directed. I was to be admitted to the hospital immediately after church. Sunday morning, as I combed my hair for the last time before it was to be shaved off for surgery on Monday, I asked the Lord why didn't he speak to me? In a still, quiet, loving tone he said; "Because I live, you can face tomorrow, because I live, all fear is gone." The fear fell down around my feet like a soiled garment. I stepped outside of the garment of fear and was anointed with a new, fresh anointing. I knew I had won the victory over the condition and the outcome no longer mattered because it was now in the hands of the Lord. Even if the Lord had decided to take me home, I know I still would have been victorious.

The surgery went well. I woke up in the recovery room many hours later, looked around me and saw regular staff people in attendance and said to myself; "This is not heaven so I must be whole." My recovery was uneventful, and I was discharged three days later. Shortly thereafter I returned to my regular duties at work. A few weeks after I returned to work, I was asked to speak at a women's prayer breakfast to testify about God's faithfulness to me, personally. Many of my co-workers came. They were still in awe of my ability to perform as if I had not undergone a critical, life threatening surgical procedure. I counted it a blessing to tell them it was not all up hill all the time but it was the end results that made the difference. My recovery was all God and none of me or anyone else. The doctors and others who aided me were instruments used by God on my behalf. I could rejoice and praise him for counting me worthy to be tested in such a manner at the conclusion of my ordeal.

Tests are different from temptations and the wrath of God. God does not tempt us, neither can he be tempted. Satan tempts us with the things we were familiar with when we were controlled by the sinful nature. God has nothing within him for sin to appeal to. He was always pure and holy. Satan lures his prey to commit unwise, immoral acts by promising them a reward that appeals to them. All temptation is orchestrated by

Satan. When we step outside of God's will for a brief moment and begin to follow our carnal thoughts and desires again, we become easy prey. Whatever we want that will bring gratification to the flesh, satisfy the lust of the eyes or involve us in the cares of the world, Satan will provide a way for us to fulfill those desires. He will build us up in pride and tell us we deserve whatever we want. There is no sin in being tempted. The sin occurs when we meditate upon the desires and the promises. We are led away by our own carnal desires.

The wrath of God is divine retribution for sin. It is not limited to the day of judgment. It is being revealed from heaven against those who, by their wickedness, suppress the truth. Not because they do not know the truth but because they chose to worship idols and other gods after they knew of the existence of God and the works of God. God gave them over to the wicked desires of their evil minds because they chose to ignore him and behave as if he did not exist. Those who degraded their bodies with each other by participating in immoral sexual activities, God gave them over to shameful lust and sexual immorality. They were also given over to depraved minds. They commit vile acts of wickedness and permit evil to prevail without fear of judgment (according to Romans 1: 18-28). Now, they cannot do any better. They probably believe what they are doing and permitting others to do is right because their minds are corrupt and morally depraved. They are not to be mistaken for crazy people. They are subtle, cunning and crafty. They know how to lure others into their web of wickedness. Many of the traits of Satan are manifested in these wicked sinners.

Believers are not immune to the attacks of Satan. When we take off the old nature with its sinful desires and put on Christ, Satan becomes very angry and begins an active campaign to lure us back to our former desires and habits. We should learn as much as we can about him and his ways of setting traps and

48

shooting fiery darts to prevent and destroy whatever good we have accomplished through Christ Jesus.

Chapter Six

WARFARE IN THE SPIRIT WORLD

The minute sinners were given a new nature they became children of God and entered the ongoing, intense battle that has been going on in the spirit world for many years. The adversary, Satan himself, makes war with God and all his children. Satan has quite a bit of power, second only to the power of God. He is a spirit and must either possess the body or influence the mind of his prey before he can operate through them. He empowers fallen angels and demon spirits to work on his behalf. We should never, ever underestimate the power and craftiness of any of them. We know that all power belongs to God, and he has empowered his children with the Holy Spirit. It is the *Spirit*, not you and me, that has power over Satan and the demon spirits. This spiritual war was perpetrated by Satan and it is fierce and constant. It is not a battle between flesh and blood human beings, so it is not fought on human terms. Our struggles are against rulers, authorities, powers of this dark world and the spiritual forces of evil in the heavenly realm (according to Ephesians 6: 12).

Satan and his demons of darkness are not overt in their approach. They camouflage themselves in attractive guise and appear as angels of light (according to 2 Corinthians 11: 14). They set traps all along the pathways believers are apt to travel frequently. If we are to avoid these traps and see through the camouflages and guises, we need a working knowledge of the modus operandi of the adversary. The battles are not against us personally although we are the targets and feel the discomforts of all the attacks from the adversary. He and his demon spirits see Christ within us. They really want to attack the spirit that dwells within us, but since they cannot do that they try to gain control of our bodies and minds. That is not to say that he does not continue to attack sinners. He is still holding them hostage to sin and he does not have to work very hard to keep them under his control. He uses sinners to influence believers to do his bidding.

The name Satan, means adversary or one who opposes another with animosity. It has been written that Satan was once an angelic being in the heavenly realm until pride filled his heart. He coveted the position of the Most High and influenced other angelic beings to join him as he made war in heaven to make his throne *like that of the Most High*. He deceived them into believing they too could be like gods. Of course he lost the battle and was judged and thrown out of heaven along with all the fallen angels. Jesus witnessed the fall of Satan from heaven which was quick, like lightning (according to Luke 10: 18). Man had not been created. The earth was permeated with darkness and was void of habitation when Satan and the angels he influenced were cast down from heaven. Angels who refused to keep their assigned positions of authority in the heavenly realm were kept in darkness. They were bound with everlasting chains for judgment on the great Day (according to Jude 6). As soon as God formed Adam and created Eve, Satan transformed himself into a serpent and beguiled her by distracting her from the command of God with pleasant conversation. When he had her undivided attention, he deceived her with the same promise he used with the fallen angels. He promised her she could be *like* God if she ate the forbidden fruit. His only interest in Eve was to use her to oppose the plan and purpose of God.

Some of Satan's characteristic traits include greed, envy, strife, deceit, murder, lying, slander, arrogance, a boastful attitude and depravity of mind. He is selfish and bold, subtle and cunning and very, very crafty. He uses provocative bribes to lure weak believers away from the will of God. He is aware of our needs and any inclinations we may have to gratify the desires of the flesh, the cravings of the eyes and the eagerness to prosper and succeed in the world. He hears our prayers, unless we pray in the heavenly language, and will put forth an effort to answer them if given the slightest opportunity. He and his demons have no loyalty or respect for anyone. Satan will try to tempt anyone who belongs to the Father, using whatever they need at the moment as bait. He made several attempts to tempt Jesus after he had fasted for forty days. He knew that Jesus must have been hungry so he tried to entice him to turn stones into bread. Every time Jesus rebuked him and refused to be tempted with one thing, Satan tried another bribe. The adversary knows believers are in a compromised position when the lines of communication between them and the Father are dead. He will come to them in whatever form necessary to get their attention. He will engage in conversation with them, and cunningly lead them away from the will, the plan and the purpose of God. He will begin to work them over quickly and thoroughly while they are out of fellowship. When the believers finally come to their senses and act upon the exigency of the Spirit and seek forgiveness, Satan is there accusing them of the very sin he enticed them to commit. He does not want God to forgive the believer and open the lines of communication again and move the believer out of adversarial territory.

There are some specific things the adversary is noted for; like preventing, destroying, stealing and killing. The thief (another name for Satan) comes only to steal and kill and destroy; I have come that they may have life and have it to the full (said Jesus in John 10: 10). The adversary's plan is to prevent the children of God from reaping as many of the benefits we received in our package deal as possible. If we do not know what we received, we will not try to collect on our inheritance. His plan is to prevent us from believing the Bible is a true account of what we need to know to glorify God. He will lead weak believers to believe something is missing from the Bible and it cannot be *totally* trusted. If he can steal the word of God from us, he can keep us ignorant of our benefits, our inheritance, and the divine purpose and the plan God has for our lives. As soon as the word is heard, Satan will steal it if it does not take root in fertile, receptive minds that believe the truths and act upon what they have heard or read in the Bible. Unless the hearer obeys the word, he is deceiving himself and is likened to a man who looks at his face in a mirror, and after looking at himself, goes away and immediately forgets what he looks like (according to James 1: 23-24). Obstacles planted by Satan can prevent believers from obeying the word if they are not focused on doing the will of the Father or if they question what they heard or read and their understanding is darkened so that they cannot grasp its truth. Those who hear the word and accept it will produce crops; thirty, sixty, and sometimes even a hundred times over what was sown (according to Mark 4: 30). It's the production of crop Satan is trying to prevent. We cannot act on the word until we accept all of it as truth. If we do not accept what we hear and read, as soon as persecution, trials and tribulations come we will fall away.

Anyone who has been born again and still more interested in worldly success and prosperity than in following God's will, can be tempted with worldly possessions and successful ideas that lead to sin and destruction. Satan can motivate spiritual leaders to teach and preach messages on prosperity without the anointing. When prosperity comes, Satan can (and does) motivate the believers he enticed to worship prosperity, to become selfish and *build bigger barns* to hold their possessions which is not what God commands. Those who are rich in this world are commanded not to be arrogant, nor put their hope in wealth, which is so uncertain. They are commanded to put their hope in God, who richly provides everything for our enjoyment. Prosperous believers should be more interested in doing good deeds by being generous and willing to share than they are in accumulating wealth. In this way, they lay up treasures for themselves as a firm foundation for the coming age so that they may take hold of the life that is truly life (according to 1 Timothy 6: 17-19). Satan is aware of how believers can use their wealth to bring glory to God but as long as he can prevent them from doing anything that glorifies God, he has accomplished his mission. Prosperity has its place in the life of believers, but it should be secondary to the will of God.

Satan would like to kill us, but since he does not have control over life and death, he attempts to kill desires for heaven, home, joy in the Lord and the spirit of love and kindness within us. If he can prevent us from believing the word, and thus from knowing and doing the will of God, he can kill the desires within us to grow. He was skillful enough to prevent the chosen people of God from entering into God's rest in the wilderness. He darkened their understanding and highlighted the things they *did not* have and *seemingly, could not* do and probably told them they should enjoy themselves a little. He influenced them to do grievous sinful deeds that brought immediate judgment upon them. This is how he works. He or his demon spirits will look for an opportunity to catch a weak, immature believer out of fellowship with the Lord. He will use attractive, inviting disguises and engage in conversation with the believer like he did with Eve. Once he has diverted their attention to him and his scheme, he will make a bet or a dare in a joking, tantalizing manner, like an offer that is hard to refuse. Once the believer begins to meditate upon the reward for winning the bet, he increases the reward and makes the bet easier to make. Once he entraps the believer in his snare he will make provisions for their sinful desires to be fulfilled. Once the sin has been committed, the believer feels guilty and the adversary tells him; "Look what the Lord made you do. If he had not given you these desires and no way to fulfill them, you wouldn't feel this way." It is a man's folly that ruins his life, yet his heart rages against the Lord (according to Proverbs 19: 3).

One of Satan's most effective tools is sexual immorality. He uses it frequently with a maximum amount of success. He has influenced the media to use sexual implications in advertising everything imaginable. He has influenced educators to preach the *gospel of condoms* instead of the true gospel of *abstinence*. They deceive the public by telling them condoms will permit them to have *safe sex*. God can prevent pregnancies and keep the diseases that devour the masses at bay. Condoms may prevent some pregnancies and occasionally some diseases but the pregnancy rate among teens and others who are unwed, has increased significantly. Sexually transmitted diseases have become lethal. Everybody is giving away free condoms, the schools, some clinics and even some churches. Is this deception or what? According to the word of God; *There is no such animal as safe sex outside of marriage!* Every believer who commits sexual intercourse and is not married is guilty of rebellion because they chose to disobey a direct command of God. Believers are to flee from sexual immorality. All other sins a man commits are outside the body, but he who sins sexually sins against his own body. Do you know that your body is a temple of the Holy Spirit, who is in you, whom you have received from God? You are not your own any more; you were bought with a very high price. Therefore you are to honor God with your body (according to 1 Corinthians 6: 18-20). The adversary influences believers to dishonor their own bodies and therefore dishonor God. There are numerous sins associated with sexual immorality. How safe from these sins can believers be if they have to deal with the wrath of God? Satan will tell us that sexual gratification is a *basic need* and there will be physical consequences if they are not satisfied, regardless of your martial status. He wants believers to think that God is not God. He does not know about *all* the needs of the very creatures he created. Don't be deceived, God will meet all your needs according to his glorious riches in Christ Jesus (according to Philippians 4: 19). The body of believers was never meant for sexual immorality, but for the Lord. All sexual interaction between anyone other than married couples is considered perverse and immoral by the Lord. Lust and ungodly desires belong to the old sinful nature believers should have left behind. The adversary will influence believers to dispute the word of God and forgo the consequences to fulfill their lustful desires. He will even tell them that God will forgive them if they confess their sins and say they are sorry. God knows the intents of the heart, he cannot be lied to, bribed or influenced in any way. He forgives us when we confess the sin as *wrong and immoral* with the intention of turning away from it. He is the embodiment of truth. A liar shall not tarry in his sight. The adversary knows the word and he will use it against believers unless believers use it against him.

Anyone who commits sexual immorality lacks judgment and destroys themselves (according to Proverbs 6: 32). We have the power to control these desires. We are to severely discipline our bodies continuously whenever they try to take control. Our bodies will come under subjection to the Spirit that dwells within us. Anyone who defames or destroys God's temple will be destroyed (according to 1 Corinthians 3: 17). While the practice of sexual immorality may not cost us our salvation, it can destroy our works, our character, and prevent us from collecting many of the rewards promised to those who obey the Lord. Every believer who is still controlled by the dark nature must ask themselves, who is on the throne of their lives? Are you being controlled by the carnal needs of the body or the Spirit of the living God? Suppose the Lord came back to claim his own while you were in the midst of an act of sexual immorality. Is that how you want him to find you? That's what Satan wants for you. We do not know when he will come. We must be ready at all times because the Son of Man will come at an hour when we do not expect him (according to Luke 12: 39).

Satan is the prince of this world and that is why many things in the world are tailored towards lustful pleasure, worldly prosperity and the desire to succeed on a worldly level. He is also prince of the demon spirits. Demons are evil spirits who do not have bodies of their own. They can transform themselves into other beings and also possess the bodies of humans. Their nature is wicked and hostile. They have nothing to lose because they have already been judged and know that at the appointed time, they will be thrown into the fiery pit that burns eternally. We should not underestimate their skills, knowledge and underhanded deceptions. They try to mimic the characteristics of God. Their deviations are so slight until it's difficult to detect them in the natural. They are good at what they do. If it was not for the Holy Spirit within us, the adversary and his demons would be able to fool the very elect of God. They know the Scriptures and will distort the meaning of passages by changing a few words here and there to make their versions seem true. They operate in hidden, devious, injurious ways, claiming to be someone that they are not. They love to disguise themselves as shepherds, teachers, prophets, evangelist and teachers. They would like to take charge of the handling of the word of God to prevent spiritual maturity and destroy the works of God in his people. Demon spirits are at work in the world in many hidden practices today.

Psychic counselors, astrologers, magicians, card readers and those who practice acts of divination are involved with demon spirits. These hostile spirits act as mediums who go between humans and the spiritual world of darkness. The mediums allegedly, reveal occult knowledge by means of supernatural agents. The demon spirits that interact between humans and the spiritual world can be influenced by whom ever they are inter-acting with. The divinators edify themselves by claiming: "I am the only one who can..." These spirits seduce the minds of those who lend themselves to their services. They look for bodies that have no spirit dwelling within to take up residence. Once they take possession of the body, they can control the entire person. Those humans whom they possess behave in violent, demonic fashions. They seemingly have no conscious and their actions are often inhumane because the spirit that controls them is not human. The demon spirits readily recognize Jesus and the power he has over them. Two demon-possessed men met Jesus as they were coming out of the tombs where they lived. They were so violent until no one could pass by the tombs. When they saw Jesus they shouted; "Son of God, what do you want with us? Have you come to torture us before our appointed time (according to Matthew 8: 28, 29)."

Perhaps the violence in our present society is due to the multitudes of demon-possessed humans we harbor. Believers who are spiritually mature have the power to cast them out. This is an intricate part of the work of the church just as healing of the sick and preaching the gospel is. Phillip, an evangelist who proclaimed the gospel at Samaria, healed the sick and cast out demons in the name of Jesus (according to Acts 8: 5-7). Spirit filled believers can do so today because the same power is still available. Only those who are certain of their new birth should attempt to cast out demons. Demon spirits can see within our beings and recognize an empty dwelling place as well as they recognize the Spirit of Jesus. Seven Jews, who were attempt-ing to drive out demons, tried to evoke the name of Jesus whom Paul preached over a demon-possessed man. The evil spirit in the man answered them saying; "Jesus I know and I know about Paul, but who are you?" The man possessed with the evil spirit jumped on them, overpowering all of them. He gave those Jews such a beating until they ran from the house naked and bleeding (according to Acts 19: 13-16). Demon Spirits fear the name and power of Jesus, but they have no fear or respect for other humans who are not filled with the Spirit of Jesus.

When evil spirits are evicted from a body by exorcism or other means except the power of the Lord, their eviction is temporary, if they leave at all. If the Spirit of the Lord does not come to dwell in the body left vacant by the evil spirit, the evil spirit will return and bring seven more spirits. Each spirit more wicked than itself, and the final condition of that man is worst than the first (according to Luke 11: 26).

No one who has received Jesus Christ into their lives should be guilty of consulting spiritual mediums or participating in the practices of anyone who uses mediums. We have access to God through Jesus Christ. He can provide us with everything we need. Consulting medium and practicing divination's is a sin. God commanded his people not to turn to other gods for any reason, ever. "Do not turn to mediums or seek out spiritualists, you will be defiled by them, I am the Lord your God. Do not practice divination's or sorcery "said the Lord (according to Leviticus 19: 31, 26). Astrologers and others who make predictions by the moon, stars or calendar are considered mediums and spiritualists. Sorcery is the same as witchcraft and magic. The dark spirits are allegedly called up by using cryptic formulas, incantations, and mystic mutterings. Divination is the art of obtaining secret knowledge, most likely pertaining to the future, in a way other than genuine prophecy by the Spirit of God.

Many believers are not aware of the wide spread influences demon spirits have on some of the people we associate with on a regular basis today. Some think that because they do not believe in demons and their power to influence believers, they cannot be seduced by them. That's just how the demon spirits would like to keep it. They want to keep their identities hidden. They prey on the innocent, the ignorant, and the inexperienced. Satan roams around the earth continuously, stealthily looking for prey. When he finds someone ignorant of his presence and his works, he pounces upon them greedily like a ravenous wolf. Humans do not have to be possessed to fall prey to his traps. All he wants to do is influence the mind. He tries to portray followers of Jesus. He may present himself as a meek, mild shepherd, coming to lead the ignorant to a place where he may obtain knowledge. His appearance and terminology may be *like* that of a true shepherd of God. He will not make the distinction as to what god he represents, knowing his prey will not ask. Beware of such, they come in sheep's clothing but inwardly they are ferocious wolves. By their fruit you will recognize them (according to Matthew 7: 15, 16). They come to distort the truth and confuse the unsuspecting. As believers, we are responsible for knowing the truth so that we cannot be easily deceived. If after knowing the truth and we choose allow to the adversary to influence us we will suffer the aftermath which follows disobedience. People *who know of* the Lord are different from people who *know* the Lord.

The question has been asked many times by many people; "Do not these false prophets, false shepherds and false teachers fear the wrath of God?" Some are united with demon spirits and have no more fear. They have already been judged and are already experiencing the wrath of God. Those who knowingly choose to respond to the knowledge of God in a rebellious way and receive pleasure from ungodly behavior, are following their own sinful will. They have already been given over to morally unprincipled minds. They are reprobates who are compelled, by their natures, to do what ought not be done. They are heartless, faithless, greedy and inconsiderate. Their hearts are darkened (according to Romans 1: 28-31).They are so wrapped up in their own conceit until they believe what they are doing and leading others to do is right. They have lived a lie so long until they cannot readily distinguish the truth from a lie. They will always find a way to justify their behavior, no matter how wicked it may be. They will never find peace and they will never be satisfied. Their egos are like consuming fires, always demanding more fuel to keep it going. There will never be enough money to please them neither will their lustful appetites ever be fulfilled. Like a consuming, fire they will always cry out for more, more, more. They will be punished along with those who practice magic arts, idolaters, cowards, unbelievers, murderers, liars and the sexual immoral. Their place will be in the fiery lake of burning sulfur (according to Revelation 21: 18). This will be the second death.

God exposed us to tests, trials and examinations and permitted us to endure the hardships to teach us how to remain strong in his mighty power. He gave us power to trample on snakes and scorpions (who represent demon spirits), and over the enemy (who is Satan himself), so that nothing would be able to harm us (according to Luke 10: 19). However, we must be alert at all times and fully dressed for battle. We must not *give* Satan and his demons any room to work in our lives. We do not fight as the world fights, we use spiritual weapons of war. Every day we should put on the following: The *belt of truth*, when everything around us seems amiss we must be held together by the Spirit of Truth that was given to us by God. Acknowledge his power and his presence. The *breast plate of righteousness,* which should keep our hearts pure and under the watchful eyes of the Lord and keep us from desiring to yield to temptation. The *gospel of peace* should cover our feet. We should see ourselves as ambassadors of Christ, taking the gospel of peace and the good news of redemption wherever we go. The *shield of faith* will give us confidence in the willingness and the capability of God to take care of us in any situation. Roman soldiers soaked their shields in water to extinguish the flaming arrows of their enemies. Our shields were soaked in the blood of Jesus on

Calvary. They still have the power to extinguish the fiery darts of the enemy. The *helmet of salvation* will protect our minds and keep us safe even if we stumble, we will not be lost. As long as we know, without a doubt, that we are kept in the safety of the Lord the adversary cannot condemn us. We are assured of our freedom from the world and on our way to eternal life. We take up *our swords*, the Bible. The word is sharp and quick like a two-edged sword it can separate and cut both ways. It can correct and reprove us as well as teach and train us. It can also be used to rebuke and resist the adversary. The word is like a mirror. When we read it and understand it we see ourselves as we are. As long as we are in the flesh, we will always see room for improvement. The word also condemns as it separates true believers from pseudo-believers.

The word is our help, our hope and the heart of our new lives. We should become as exceedingly familiar with it as money handlers who handle large volumes of bills are in detecting counterfeit bills. They can feel a bill and distinguish the counterfeit bills from the real ones almost immediately. Visual examination of a counterfeit bill enables them to verify the difference effectively and efficiently. One way to differentiate between what is real and what is counterfeit is frequent handling of the real. When we see and hear the word of God and allow it to touch us, on a consistent basis, we will be able to readily discern the difference between the real truth and the counterfeit. When we become immensely familiar with the word we will question the counterfeit and the counterfeiter.

There is assurance in knowing that God will not permit the adversary to tempt us with anything strange and uncommon to mankind. God will also give us the strength to stand up under the temptations without yielding to any of them. Above all, he will provide a means of escape for us (according to 1 Corinthians 10: 13). If we submit to God, we can resist the adversary and he will leave us quickly, but only for a season. He will return time and time again. All we have to do is submit to the Lord and resist him each time he comes and he will leave quickly every time.

We have learned a portion of what we need to know to become Christians, but we are still in the midst of spiritual labor pains. We are already in the spiritual delivery room but *The Birth of a Christian* has not yet come to pass.

Chapter Seven

THE BIRTH OF A CHRISTIAN

God created us to love him back in return for the matchless love he has always felt for us. He wanted a two-way relationship, based on divine love between him and all mankind. He wanted someone to make a decision to love him because they wanted to. That's why he created us as free moral agents, so he would know that we chose to love him back. It was out of love that he created Adam and molded Eve. Love is one of God's essential attributes. He created us in his image and gave us some of his characteristic traits. We are like him in that we want someone to make a decision to love us just because they want to. He had that kind of relationship with Adam and Eve in the beginning. That wonderful relationship remained intact for quite some time. Adam and Eve looked forward to the visits from the Lord in the cool of the evening. The Lord enjoyed the visits as well. The angels delighted in looking down upon God as he interacted with his loved ones. Then one day Eve and Adam chose to follow the evil seductions of the serpent over the divine command of the Lord their God! Oh, this made God exceedingly unhappy. His special loved ones whom he had created with his own hands, showered with unparalleled love and made provisions to supply them with everything they needed, had chosen to follow another. God knew the one they chose to disobey him for was no good for them. Their seducer only wanted to destroy them. He would never, ever have their best

64

interest in mind because his nature was evil and selfish.

We respond to rejection in like manner. When someone we love dearly and shower with attention and precious gifts, chooses to be seduced by someone else, we become hurt, disappointed and even angry, especially when we know that the one they chose over us will not do right by them. We, like God, want devotion and a lasting commitment from those whom we choose to love.

When man made that dreadful decision to sin, God did not stop loving him. All believers are eternally grateful that God did not turn his back and walk away, leaving mankind at the mercy of Satan throughout eternity. Although Adam and Eve had to pay retribution for the sin of disobedience, God immediately made plans for the birth of a Christian to occur. He wanted them back without the stains of sin and the guilt of the curse Satan had left upon them. He wanted mankind to be with him throughout eternity. *That's true love, unconditional and matchless.*

Jesus Christ was the vehicle through which the broken relationship and fellowship was to be restored. The birth of a Christian will take place when we become true imitators of Christ all day, every day. Everything that God made was to produce after its own kind. We were born of Jesus Christ and we are to produce lives that parallel his life while he was on earth. The restoration of the relationship between God and man, and between man and God was to restore the two-way love connection just as it was before the fall. The growth and development of believers is for the purpose of enabling us to walk in the steps of our Savior while we remain in the world. *Christians follow Christ,* that's why we were saved and that's why we are to be called Christians. How do we follow Christ and where do we begin?

We now have the essential nature of God which is divine love. Following Jesus means doing the things he did. Our attention should not be on *pleasing self* any longer. Our hearts and souls should be focused on pleasing God. Just as Christ loved us and gave himself as a fragrant offering and sacrifice to God we are to begin by imitating his sacrificial love (according to Ephesians 5: 1, 2). You are probably saying to yourself; "Does she mean give up my life?" When the Christian is born in your heart it will be a privilege to sacrifice your life for the sake of the Savior and for the sake of the gospel. When you have learned about sacrificial love, and begin to live as if you are just passing through this world , you will know that you have moved out of the birth canal and entered into a new exciting spiritual experience. We will remain in the spiritual birth canal waiting to be delivered until we learn how to experience sacrificial love as a way of live.

The *nucleus* of Christianity is divine love which comes down from the Father. It was the Father's unconditional love for us that motivated him to send his only Son down to earth and have him undergo an extraterrestrial metamorphosis from pure Spirit so he could become physical (in human form) so that we could be transformed from natural to spiritual. Jesus underwent such a change because of his love for the Father as well as his love for us. He knew we were still his enemies because we were dead in sins but that did not stop him because his love was without conditions. This was the first time deity had ever been clothed in flesh. Because he knows what it means to suffer because he suffered when he was tempted, Jesus is able to help others who are being tempted out of love and familiarity (according to Hebrews 2:17). Before delivery of a Christian can be completed in our lives we must be motivated by the same kind of love which will give birth to obedience like Jesus displayed.

Salvation and Christianity are not the same. One can be saved and never live the life of a true Christian. As we know, salvation is the process that begins with the new birth, and is made complete when we take off the mortal flesh completely and clothe ourselves in immortality so that we can live with the Lord

66

forever. What we will be at that time is not fully known yet. We know that when the Lord appears, we will be like him (according to 1 John 3: 2). A Christian is a believer who follows the doctrines and the examples of Christ and *always* does the will of the Father. It becomes a new way of life, mirroring the life of Christ Jesus, while we remain in our mortal bodies. Our sacrificial love will be manifested in our attitudes and our works. Christians live as if Jesus is coming back within the next blinking of an eye. Christian's lives are pure just as the Lord is pure. Their hope is built on the eternal things, like eternal salvation and the peerless opportunity to see the Lord as he is (according to 1 John 3: 3). This goal becomes the reason for living.

Hope is more than wishful thinking. It's a deeply embedded longing or heart-felt desire with unchangeable confidence that what we hope for will come to pass. We are so certain of the ability of God to make possible, whatever we hope for until we diligently look for it and rejoice in the hope before what we desire has been fulfilled. Our hope is not empty, but based on the word and he who inspired the word. Such assurance motivates us to prepare ourselves for the presentation through purification. We make a conscious decision to turn away from *everything* unclean and morally wrong. We turn to something better to take the place of our former habits. Believers with unwavering hope turn to the object of their love, the Lord Jesus himself. We endeavor to love like he loves. To love like Jesus loves, we must *know* divine love in our inner most selves, what it is and how it can be made manifest in our daily lives.

Try as we may, we cannot come up with a stable definition for love that represents all love really is. Affection and strong attraction are much too weak to embody the spiritual, emotional and life changing impact love has. We know that it is an essential attribute of God and is a preeminent virtue in the life of a Christian. We know the test of discipleship is also a way of testing our love. But does that tell us what love is? The

Scripture says this is how we know what love is: Jesus Christ laid down his life for us, and we ought to lay down our lives for our brother (according to 1 John 3: 16). Are we giving up our lives again? Who are the brothers for whom we are supposed to be giving up our lives? Jesus told his disciples that whoever does the will of his Father is his brother. We are to follow his example. Our brother is anyone who believes in the incarnate Christ (that he came in human, bodily form). Those who follow the doctrines and examples of Jesus and encourage us to do the same are our brothers. Believers who are united in fellowship through Jesus Christ in love are our brothers. Our brothers love Jesus Christ as he loves them. That love is made manifest when those brothers who have possessions see other brothers in need and have pity on them and share their possessions with them, just like Jesus Christ did. There is a loving relationship and loving fellowship among brothers who are members of the body of Christ. It's not so hard to imagine having sacrificial love for someone whom we trust will have the same kind of love for any other member of the household of faith.

Everyone born of God are partakers of the divine love that is his essential nature. When we show love for one another it affirms that God lives in us and his love is made complete in us (according to 1 John 4: 7, 15). The more mature we become in love the more of the Father's traits are made manifest in our lives. When we think of sacrificial love in a natural sense, we may decide that we cannot go that far. We reason the matter out in our limited minds and think, there can only be one sacrifice for salvation, that has already occurred. What would it prove if I gave my life since there can be only one Jesus? Although we are no longer citizens of this world, many of us still think of life only in the tangible, physical sense.

What is physical life and what does it mean to us? Life represents the sum total of all our mental, physical and spiritual experiences. *We* determine the importance of each experience and categorize each one. We have many meaningful life experiences and each one passes on, never to return again. No matter how good or important the experience was, we can never retrieve it again. Sane, highly intelligent people get high on cocaine, seeking new experiences. The initial high (is said to) gives them a once in a lifetime experience. They become addicted and lose everything including their lives sometimes, in search of that initial high again. Needless to say, they never retrieve it. We should have taken off the natural life in the flesh by now, which is essentially what we are trying to cling to. Life, the way it was designed by our Creator to be, belongs to the Lord (according to Deuteronomy 30:20). Whether we live or die, prosper or not, produce or remain nonproductive is all determined by the Lord. A Christian is born within us when our present life is not too much to sacrifice for the sake of the Lord. Life for a Christian, in the robe of flesh, becomes a burden as the heart longs for heaven and home. If for some reason, the Lord appoints us to sacrifice our lives, we ought to love him enough to be willing and obedient enough to do so without question. It's part of the *"fellowship"* of Christ Jesus. He said; "If anyone would come after me, he must deny himself, and take up his cross and follow me. For whoever wants to save his life will lose it, but whoever loses his life for me and for the gospel will save it." What good is it for a man to gain the whole world and lose his soul? (Mark 8: 35, 36). Physical life should become secondary to eternal life. This can only happen when the love of God and the hope of seeing him as he is overshadows any experience we may have in the flesh. When we make a steadfast decision to follow Christ Jesus all the way to the cross if necessary, we will have a burning desire to go where he went, do what he did and live in him and just fill our beings with the love of him.

We often quote the verse of Scripture that says: "Greater things than these will you do when the Holy Spirit has come."

Sometimes we quote it to make a point. Other times we are trying to invoke a blessing or prove to others how strong we are
in the word, especially if we are not living up to his name. All
of us are capable of doing great things. We must be willing to
do *some* of the many things Jesus did and the things he *commanded* before we try to do *greater* things? Jesus' journey was
not filled with joy and glad tidings. Following him is not confined to healing the sick, raising the dead and receiving blessings that we do not have enough room to receive. Review his
entire journey on earth. He went through some valleys and met
some vicious, evil, strong willed, self-righteous people and had
some lonely days. He did not own a home or possess any other
luxuries that worldly prosperity provides. He was persecuted,
ridiculed and even killed because he refused to pacify the
worldly leaders. Christians transcend the natural realm of things
and live in the spiritual realm, just as Jesus did.

This is how we learn to walk with Christ. We begin to see
ourselves in heavenly places, where God already sees us. We
are to rejoice when we suffer for the sake of Christ Jesus and the
gospel, instead of grumbling and complaining when the least little thing goes wrong. We become completely humble and gentle. We become patient; bearing with one another in love. We
make every effort to keep the unity of the Spirit through the bond
of peace (according to Ephesians 4: 2-3). Followers of Christ
put off falsehood and speak truthfully to their neighbors. They
refuse to let any unwholesome talk come out of their mouths,
but only what is helpful for building others up according to their
needs. We do not grieve the Holy Spirit of God with whom we
are sealed for the day of redemption. We rid ourselves of all bit-
terness, rage and anger, slander and brawling along with every
form of malice. Christ's followers are kind and compassionate
to one another, forgiving each other just as in Christ, God for-
gave them (according to Ephesians 4: 25, 29-32).

The world will hate us, because we are not of this world,

just like Jesus was not. Are we greater than Jesus was? They persecuted Jesus so they will persecute us for his namesake (according to John 15: 20, 21). *Christians are Christ's namesake.* We do not have to welcome persecution, but it is all involved in the life of a Christian. We are to accept it and rejoice for the privilege of being persecuted for his name sake. When we think about sacrificing our lives as Jesus sacrificed his life, most of us look for other ways to show divine love to make up for the lack of wanting to give up our lives. Very few of us are ever ready to die. It is a hard thing to think about even for some mature Christians. Usually we think we have so much unfinished business. We begin to meditate on what we think we are leaving behind, instead of what awaits us in glory. You are probably saying, "Jesus did not want to die either." Jesus did not agonize over the physical pain he was going to suffer, neither over shedding the flesh that caused him to suffer. He agonized over the thought of being separated from his Father. He did not love this present world that much. We should be happy to take of this heavy robe of troublesome flesh. Giving birth to a Christian is a laborious experience.

As believers, we should view death differently from the world because we are sure where we will spend eternity. When God appoints us to die, I do not believe we will be unprepared. Christians no longer fear death because there is no fear in love. Perfect love drives our fear. Fear is associated with torment and punishment such as sinners will receive (according to 1 John 4: 8). Christians will be rewarded, not punished or tormented. Death has long since lost its sting and the grave has lost its victory. Jesus took care of all that when he descended into hell.

I worked on a Gynecology-Oncology Unit as a nursing care coordinator for a number of years where I witnessed numerous deaths. Very few of our patients faced death with fear or torment, especially those who were certain of their future. It was my duty to prepare them to make the transition from the *lower form of life to a higher form of life.* One patient's experience was especially special to me. I will call her Mrs. Faith. She was diagnosed many years before her body began to show signs of debilitation. When she was first diagnosed, she had a ninety percent chance of a cure, if she had consented to have surgery. However, her husband (influenced by his father) forbade her to have the surgery. Her disease progressed beyond our ability to help her over a period of years. She underwent many painful, physical changes and became progressively bitter and hard to deal with for the regular staff. She and I became very close since I chose to care for her most of the time. Her disease had metastasized to other organs including her bowels and bones. It was extremely painful for her to stretch out her legs and turn from one side to the other. Her skin had taken on a dark ashen tone and she moaned and groaned a lot. I talked with her often about forgiveness and making peace with her transgressors and then with God. Over a period of years she made peace with her transgressors, herself and God. One morning she called for me to come to her room as soon as I arrived in my office. When I went to her room, she didn't need anything or even want to talk. She just asked me to sit in the chair next to her bed. An uncanny quietness, likened to a hush, fell over the room. Mrs. Faith's skin tone began to take on a colorful, healthy glow. She stretched out her legs without the usual out cry of pain, closed her eyes and gave a deep sigh as she slipped into another dimension of life. I thought for sure I heard the flutter of wings and the voice of angels singing over her head. Whether the fluttering and the voices were in my spirit or not, I cannot say. I did see that Mrs. Faith had been restored to her original beauty. She had invited me to share in the greatest experience of life I have ever encountered. For a few minutes, I just sat there spell bound. I do not believe I could have moved if I so desired. The experience was indeed spiritual and it was awesome to witness! I felt as if I had just witnessed the transformation from one life form to another.

I do not know what holy ground feels like, but if I had to define it, it would have been that experience in that patient's room.

Physical death for a Christian is the final victory over the flesh. A Christ-like attitude of love can be manifested even in death as we humbly submit to the calling of our Lord and Savior.

Humbleness was another attitude Jesus displayed throughout his physical life, even as he died on the cross. Humbleness is by no means synonymous with weakness. Christians are not meant to become the doormats of the world. It takes a strong, well adjusted, assured person to take on an attitude of humbleness. Humbleness denotes the presence of gentleness and quietness within the soul and the absence of arrogance and pride. It is expressed by an attitude of submissiveness and obedience to God out of love and respect. To rid ourselves of arrogance and pride, our whole state of mind has to be made new. We put off all carnal desires, habits and traits of the old self like we are shedding soiled garments. They have no place in the life of a Christian. When we take off the old we can put on the new self created to be like the Lord, in true righteousness and holiness (according to Ephesians 4: 24). As we submit to the guidance of the Holy Spirit, he will enable us to undress and redress ourselves to fit the standards of righteousness that bring glory to God. The new self, created in righteousness, will be made manifest in our daily lives. We will appreciate the outcome of trials, tests and life experiences. The severe disciplining of our bodies will produce holy temples controlled by the Spirit. As we grow we will depend more and more on the Lord and less and less on self, which will increase our faith. When our lives are completely hidden with Christ in God our minds are focused on things that are in heaven instead of things on earth. We can imitate Christ in our daily walk because we no longer regard life in the flesh as important as we regard life in the spirit.

Although Jesus was God by nature, he did not flaunt his

deity in the faces of his enemies with pride and arrogance. Instead, he disrobed himself of his glory and made himself nothing, taking on the role of a servant. This was a sign of lowering his status as a totally submissive servant of the Father. He did the will of the father all the time without murmuring and complaining. He endured the ridicule and persecution of worldly administrators of justice to fulfill his purpose for coming in the flesh. In humble submission, he endured the death on the cross, a type of punishment reserved for those who committed vile crimes. Criminals who died on the cross were taunted and humiliated by all who passed by as they hung there in sheer agony. Jesus never attempted to defend himself or repay his tormentors in any way. He asked the Father to forgive them because they could not grasp the concept of what they were doing.

Following his last act of love, obedience, humility and submission in the flesh, Jesus was exalted to the highest place there is and given a name above every name. Every knee must bow and every tongue must someday confess that Jesus is Lord. If we remain steadfast all the way to the end, we will be rewarded in accordance with our works. Only those works that glorified God will be considered. Remember, the race is not given to the fastest runner, nor the battle to the ones with more physical strength (according to Ecclesiastes 9: 11). The crown will be given to those who endure until the end.

Love, self-sacrifice, obedience, submission and humility are the hallmarks of Christianity. If we followed the life of Jesus as it is outlined in the word we would know that he led a peculiar life. He did not engage in foolishness, neither did he participate in anything sinful. As we approach the reality of the birth of Christian we must become peculiar with singleness of mind. God has given us *road* signs that we must observe as we travel up and down the different pathways in our new lives. Our journey will lead us beside still waters and up paths of righteousness already made straight by our trust in the Lord. Sometimes though, we may have to climb up rough sides of mountains and travel down winding roads of distress. If we listen to the voice of the Spirit he will keep our feet from slipping and prevent us from falling. In the natural, we have no problem observing the signs of the road as we travel from one place to another on the world's highways. We obey the road signs out of fear, habit and the consequences of violating the laws of the land. We make a conscious effort to observe all of them and even commit them to memory. When the signal lights flashes to red, we burn rubber trying to stop before entering the cross-walk. When automated signs for pedestrians say "Do not walk," we jump back on the curb and wait for a command to walk before we proceed. Red stationary stop signs command our attention and obedience. The consequences of disobeying the warnings and commands of the living God greatly exceed the consequences of disobeying man made laws.

God's road signs are in the form of warnings and commands aimed at separating his children from the children of the world. Some of them are: *do not, refrain from, avoid, flee, turn away from, resist and you should not*; there are others that you will recognize as you travel through the word but these are enough to give you an idea of what to expect. The Holy Spirit will warn us when we are about to violate one of the Lord's commands. We should diligently seek to follow his commands and immediately turn off any road that will lead to sin. The spirit of the adversary is at work in those who disobey the Lord's commands (according to Ephesians 2: 2). Don't be deceived, God cannot be mocked. Everyone reaps what they sow. Anyone who rejected the Law of Moses died without mercy on the testimony of two or three witnesses. How much more severely do you think a man deserves to be punished who tramples the Son of God underfoot, who has treated as an unholy thing the blood covenant that sanctified him, and who insulted the Spirit of grace? For we know him who says; "It is mine to avenge, I will pay," and again, "the Lord will judge his people." It is a dreadful thing to fall into the hands of the living God (according to Hebrews 10: 28-31). As long as we observe the commands and heed the warnings, we will not fall into the hands of the living God. However, as incomprehensible as God's love is for his children, and as much as he wants to see us reap the benefits of the rewards he has in store for us, he will not share us with the adversary. He is a jealous God who requires total devotion in worship and obedience to his commands. We no longer belong to ourselves to do what we please. We have no right to disrespect God by disobeying his commands and ignoring his warnings. He moves mountains and leads us around stumbling blocks. He commands unseen angels to keep a constant watch over us. He takes very good care of us, but makes it very clear that we cannot be of God and of the world at the same time. We must make a definite choice. Failure to choose to follow Christ can only result in catering to the world and all the filth, deception and sin it has to offer. Whatever or whomever we choose becomes our god. We cannot serve idols and the Lord at the same time. The closer we come to complete deliverance the more steadfast the adversary will become in his attempts to prevent us from receiving total fulfillment in the Lord.

Have we come to the place where we can make a steadfast decision to follow Christ Jesus all the way to the cross if that becomes necessary? Our question is always the same, how can we do this? We begin by worshipping the Lord our God with all that we are. We worship him with our bodies, our minds, our hearts. Everything we do, think and say should bring glory to him. In view of his mercy, we offer our bodies as living sacrifices, holy and pleasing to him as our spiritual act of worship (according to Romans 12: 1). We do this by treating our bodies as temples where the Spirit of God lives. We no longer see the real person we have become as flesh, but as purified creations of the Lord, sacred, to be used by him in whatever way he deems essential. When we begin to live like Christians, some of our close friends and family members may think we are acting strange. They may attempt to lure us back into the world because we are no longer fun to be around in the worldly sense. We should offer them Jesus and the opportunity for a new life. If they refuse to allow the word of God to change them, we may have to part company with them until we have things in common with them again (hoping and praying for their conversion). Christianity is a personal, lifetime commitment. Our spiritual lives depend on it. Our fellowship should be with other believers who love the Lord like we do and are actively following his doctrines. We are to become one with other members of the *body of Christ* who are fulfilling God's purpose and doing God's will in their daily lives. We share with others who are less fortunate from the storehouse of plenty God has provided for us. We share our best as if we were sharing with God. Whatever we do for others is not done in pride so we do not boast about it. We become devoted to pleasing the Lord in every aspect of our lives.

To walk with Christ Jesus, our priorities must change, sometimes drastically. Our primary goal in life becomes the same as Jesus' goal was when he walked this earth, to do the will of the Father. We empty ourselves of everything and become filled again with the Spirit. The people we once were no longer exist; they are now dead. Therefore, they can neither dictate to us any longer nor have any control over our new lives. We are indeed, new creations in Christ. The Father will not compete with our will for position. Our love for God, self-sacrifice, humility, devotion and obedience must come from a willing heart. We are to become submissive by yielding our will as often as it gets in the way of our devotion to the Lord. To remain in God's will we empty our minds continuously and stay in a position of reformation. Reformation brings about transformation on the inside which is reflected on the outside. We are coming to one of God's road signs that directs us in the right pathway. Do not conform to the patterns of this world any longer, but be transformed by the renewing of your mind on a day to day basis. Then you can test and approve what God's will is; his good, pleasing and perfect will (according to Romans 12: 2). We renew our minds through the word of God. If we are still practicing worldly traits and habits, we are to stop immediately. Failure to stop at this warning signal will result in a mandatory appearance before the Judge. Consequences consistent with acts of rebellion and disobedience will be handed down.

If we want to know what God's will is for the believer, we must search the Scriptures where God will always reveal exactly what he wants us to do. When our minds have been renewed and transformed we can hear him clearly. His revelations may not always be what we want to hear but they will always be something that will please him and bring glory to him. Following his will is the only way to continue our walk with Christ Jesus. We grow as we walk. One way to make sure you are in God's will is to develop an interpersonal relationship with him. Be available to talk to him and listen when he talks back.

Whenever I am looking for spiritual guidance, I read Proverbs 3: 5. That scripture says, "Trust in the Lord with all your heart, lean not to your own understanding in all your ways acknowledge him and he will make your paths straight." I experienced the validity of that passage about six years ago. I wanted an excuse not to keep a promise to my sister Mary, about going back to our hometown for a class reunion with her. I prayed believing the Lord would point out how senseless this trip would be for me since I had just taken a vacation the month before. He gave me Proverbs 3: 5. Well, I didn't know how to connect this to what I was asking him so I said; "Well Lord, if you want me to go make some provisions for me." He quickly provided me with funds in abundance. He also made a way for me to get an airline ticket at a discount rate although the airline's sale had expired two days before I purchased my ticket. Whatever I asked him along the way the answer was always Proverbs 3: 5. While I was at the reunion I was asked to counsel with an oncology patient I had never met. It turned out to be a spiritual encounter controlled by the Holy Spirit. I also met my husband on that trip. God obviously appointed the trip for me in advance. If I had failed to commit to him and his wisdom, I would have missed two wonderful blessings. I recently received a revelation about God's will for me from Proverbs 3:5. I would like to share the revelation with you now.

I was asking the Lord, how do I trust with all my heart without allowing what I understand to influence my thinking? This was what I received. Dedicate your mind to the Lord, totally. Begin every day in dedication with the idea, "I know nothing but God knows everything." Then I wanted to know how to acknowledge him. I already knew of his existence and such as I was capable of knowing about his greatness, that to me, is too wonderful for words. This is what I received. Make the confession aloud, of his wonderful existence as All Truth. He also reminded me to draw on *my* personal knowledge I had of him within my own heart. Believe, no matter what my intellect tried to dictate, if I asked *anything within his will* in sincerity and righteousness he would respond. Maybe not like I expected but he would respond. I knew within my heart that I did not know what to do, where to go or how to get there and do it all in God's will. His plan permitted me to cast all my anxieties upon him. I designated a special place in the house to talk with the Lord daily. I began to read a chapter of the Bible each morning as the Spirit directed me (mostly books from Psalm). Following the reading of the word I was usually in an attitude of praise and gratitude. I began to humble myself before the Lord and get down on my knees to pray. At the end of my prayer I began to ask the Lord to make my pathway straight for today. Sometimes

I began to just ask for today's assignment. I began to remain on my knees, still and quiet, until the Lord responded, telling me what path to take for the day. He does not always answer immediately but he always answers. I have experienced some powerful directives in my day to day life by following this principle. Sometimes the telephone will ring before I get out of bed and I jump up and go about my day. When I find myself spinning my wheels, I realize that I have no direction. I immediately stop and have a talk with the Lord. On one such day I was trying to get out of the house and just could not get it together. I made an attempt to just walk out of the door anyway and leave whatever I was forgetting undone when a voice inside of me said; "Where are going, you have no assignment?" I laughed and went back, read the Bible, prayed and waited for my assignment. My directives were totally different from what I had in mind to do but whatever I did was productive. It's so rewarding to know that we are in God's will. Even when we do not know where we are going, it's comforting to know that we have total confidence in our Guide. After all, our purpose for living should be to please God. When we are doing what he wants us to do we are pleasing him. *The Birth of a Christian* can be realized when we are in God's will and live in Christ Jesus and make his place within us holy. Our bodies become temples that he will be delight with and in. We form a living union with Christ and live there every day, under all kinds of conditions.

As we know by now, *the birth of a Christian* is a laborious process, lasting much longer than the birth of a natural child. Before the final act of delivery takes place and we become worthy of wearing the name of *Christian* we must bear the heartaches and the pains of labor. There has to be fair amount of pushing by the Spirit as we endeavor to give up or stop trying before reaching the ultimate goal. We will do breathing exercises as we sigh when given rest periods from weariness and pant when in distress. When the cord is finally cut, separating us from the world that we made ourselves comfortable in, we will begin to live above circumstances without looking back. Once we hear the *Spirit cry* with relief within us, we, like natural mothers will quickly forget the labor pains, will do so too and embrace the Lord Jesus Christ. We will hold him close to our breasts like mothers caress their children. We will know that he is ours and we are his. At the moment, the Christian within us is delivered. A bond stronger than life and more powerful than death will be formed, and we can join the writer in Romans 8: 35-37 and say; "Who can separate us from the love of Christ? Shall trouble or hardship or persecution or famine or nakedness or danger or sword? No, in all these things we are more than conquerors through him who loved us. For I am convinced that neither death nor life, neither angels nor demons, neither the present nor the future, nor any powers, neither height nor depth, nor anything else in all creation, will be able to separate us from the love of God that is in Christ Jesus our Lord.

As long as we live in the Spirit we will continue to offer to God, sacrifices of praise, the fruit of the lips that confess his name. And not forget to do good and share with others, for with such sacrifices, God is pleased (according to Hebrews 13: 15-16). May God richly bless and keep you as you give birth to a Christian within your heart.

Chart Your Progress

Chart Your Progress

Chart Your Progress

BOOKS AVAILABLE THROUGH
Milligan Books
By Dr. Rosie Milligan

The Birth of A Christian, $9.95

Rootin' For The Crusher, $12.95

Temptation - $12.95

Collection of Conscious Poetry - 9.95

Negroes-Colored People-Blacks-African-Americans in America- $13.95

Starting A Business Made Simple - $20.00

Getting Out of Debt Made Simple - $20.00

Nigger, Please -14.95

A Resourse Guide for African American Speakers & Writers - 49.95

...............................**Order Form**.....................................

Mail Check or Money Order to: 1425 W. Manchester, suite B, Los Angeles, CA 90047

Name_____Date_____

Address_____

City_____State _____Zip Code_____

Day Telephone _____

Eve Telephone _____

Name of book(s) _____

Sub Total $ _____

Sales Tax (CA) Add 8.25% $ _____

Shipping & Handling $3.00 $ _____

Total Amount Due $ _____

❑ Check   ❑ Money Order

❑ Visa   ❑ Master Card   Ex. Date _____

Credit Card No. _____

Driver's License No. _____

_____   _____

Signature   **Date**